HITTING BACK
*An Austrian Jew
in the French Résistance*

published in cooperation with
THE AVRAHAM HARMAN INSTITUTE
OF CONTEMPORARY JEWRY
THE HEBREW UNIVERSITY OF JERUSALEM

HITTING BACK

An Austrian Jew in the French Résistance

by
Dolly Steindling

Introduction, Epilogue, and Annotations
by HAIM AVNI

edited by
HAIM AVNI AND SUSANNA STEINDLING

UNIVERSITY PRESS OF MARYLAND

LIBRARY OF CONGRESS CATALOGING-IN-PUBLICATION

Steindling, Dolly.
  [Vinah, Tsarefat, Vinah. English]
  Hitting back : an Austrian Jew in the French resistance / Dolly Steindling ; introduction, epilogue, and annotations by Haim Avni.
    p. cm. — (Studies and texts in Jewish history and culture ; 6)
  ISBN 1-883053-53-6
    1. Steindling, Dolly. 2. Jews—Austria—Vienna—Biography. 3. Communists—Austria—Vienna—Biography. 4. Refugees, Jewish—France—Biography. 5. World War, 1939–1945—Jewish resistance—France—Personal narratives. 6. Vienna (Austria)—Biography. I. Avni, Haim. II. Title. III. Series.

DS135.A93 S74713 2000
943.6'13004924'0092—dc21
[B]   99-053812

Translated from the German by
Andrew Clark-Wilson

Restyled by
Heather Rockman

Cartography by Tamar Soffer

Cover design by Duy-Khuong Van

Copyright © 2000 by H. Avni and S. Steindling. All rights reserved. This book may not be reproduced, in whole or in part, in any form (beyond that copying permitted in Sections 107 and 108 of the U.S. Copyright Law and except by reviewers for the public press), without written permission from the publisher, University Press of Maryland, P.O. Box 34454, Bethesda, Md. 20827.

STUDIES AND TEXTS IN JEWISH HISTORY AND CULTURE

The Joseph and Rebecca Meyerhoff Center
for Jewish Studies
University of Maryland

VI

General Editor: Bernard D. Cooperman

UNIVERSITY PRESS OF MARYLAND

STUDIES AND TEXTS IN JEWISH HISTORY AND CULTURE

I

Religion and Politics in the Ancient Near East
A. Berlin, Editor

II

Freedom and Moral Responsibility: General and Jewish Perspectives
C. H. Manekin, Editor

III

Land and Community: Geography in Jewish Studies
H. Brodsky, Editor

IV

A Life in Jewish Education: Essays in Honor of Louis L. Kaplan
J. Fruchtman, Jr., Editor

V

Religious and Ethnic Communities in Later Roman Palestine
H. Lapin, Editor

VI

Hitting Back: An Austrian Jew in the French Résistance
Dolly Steindling (H. Avni and S. Steindling, Editors)

VII

The Jews of Italy: Memory and Identity
B. D. Cooperman and B. Garvin, Editors

VIII

The Six-Day War and World Jewry
H. Avni, S. DellaPergola, E. Lederhendler, and G. Shimoni, Editors

IX

Rememberings:
The World of a Russian-Jewish Woman in the Nineteenth Century
Pauline Wengeroff
(H. Wenkart, Translator; B. D. Cooperman, Editor)

Table of Contents

INTRODUCTION

ix

REFUGEE

Vienna, The Anschluss, Departure	3
The Road to Switzerland	14
From Zurich to France	18
Paris	25
The Refugee's Reality	31
Belgium	37
French Concentration Camps	43
Gurs	58
Agricultural "Training"	68
The Flight from Rosans	77

IN THE *RÉSISTANCE*

Escape from a Shelter	91
Hitler's "Fortress Europe"	100
Conflicting Identities: Steindling and Obrecht	108
Obrecht's Adventures	119
Arrest	126
Prisoner of the Gestapo	139
The Flight	151
Back to Activity	157
The Surgery	165
Confession	176

Hitting Back

In the *Maquis*	181
Fighting in Tournon	190
Liberated France	198
The Road to Austria	207
Back in Vienna	216

EPILOGUE
222

NOTES
228

Introduction

THE AUSTRIAN AND FRENCH CONTEXTS, THE JEWISH ASPECTS

"Dolly," a name commonly given to the female sex, was the nickname of our author — Adolf (Aaron) Steindling — since his early childhood. It was this name, in fact, that saved his life in 1944: when the Gestapo uncovered the network of activists in the Austrian resistance in Lyon and Vienna and "Dolly" was one of the names on their list, it was a woman they searched for. This fateful event in the history of the Austrian resistance movement is described, among others, in this extensive personal document.

THE MEMOIR

The manuscript was found among the author's papers upon his death in 1983. He had begun writing it early in 1978 at his home in Vienna and during his frequent travels and completed it some two and a half years later. It was not intended for publication, neither was it written to serve as a "moralistic" testimony to his daughters or his extended family. No remarks or implicit hints of such an intention could be found in the text. Moreover, the occasional mention of his amorous liaisons, including one with an outspoken Nazi girl when he worked under cover as a French Alsatian, exclude the possibility of such a purpose. Why did he write this memoir? He asked himself this question, pondered about it, and continued his annotations.

The author apparently used very few sources to substantiate his recollections. On September 4, 1945, he wrote a long and detailed letter to his parents who had settled in Israel (at that time Palestine) shortly before the war broke out. He summarized what had transpired since their parting at the Friedensbruecke ("Bridge of Peace") in Vienna in the early summer of 1938. In 1965, two years after the establishment of the *Dokumentationsarchiv des österreichischen Widerstandes*, he provided a short description of his activities in the Austrian resistance movement in an interview for the archives, and in 1976 included an even more concise version in his letter to the French *Ministère des Anciens Combattants et Victimes de la Guerre*. These documents, along with a few comments jotted down on small slips of paper as names and events came to mind, are the only written material yielded by his own files and those of the Austrian archives. In December 1979, while writing about the clash between his adopted identity ("Jean Obrecht") and his real identity (p. 108), he granted an interview to a young American Jewish journalist who was writing a book about the experience of Jews who survived the Holocaust disguised as Christians.[1] During eight hours of tape recording, Dolly Steindling summarized what he had already written by that time. However, in responding to the interviewer's questions he delved even deeper into his introspective recollections. Our review of the recordings showed that although he disclosed only those factual details that he considered relevant to the interviewer's interest, or suitable to his understanding of the events, the interview actually enriched the contemplative aspects of his written testimony.

Introduction

In terms of its documentary value, these reminiscences should be regarded as an outstanding meld of autobiography and oral history. With autobiographies, where the goal is usually publication, the authors are concerned with their image and reputation in the eyes of readers and try to provide their version of what should be kept in the common memory. In contrast, this memoir was not written with such a purpose. It does not even locate the author at a focal point of the larger "historical" events. Thus it maintains the characteristics of a spontaneous and detached account. In oral history we usually strive to lead our interviewees to "relive" — in the fullest detail — the events and scenes they are describing. In his writings Dolly Steindling did precisely that: he relived those experiences in the most intensive way by describing them in vivid detail. The comparison between his written memoirs and the recordings of his oral history sessions with the journalist place the manuscript at the highest point of a carefully reviewed and expanded transcription of an oral history document.

Oral documentation is always most valuable when the testimony refers to deeds and events that have no parallel existing archival written documents. This memoir complies thoroughly with this basic criterion.

The Austrian and French Contexts

Dolly Steindling's testimony bears evidence to a sequence of events that took place on four "stages" and are set in chronological order. The first is that of refugee life in Switzerland, France, and Belgium, before and during the "phony war" (March 1938 – May 1940) and in the French concentration camps Saint Cyprien and Gurs in the south of France (June 1940 to August

1942). The second stage refers to the *Travail Anti-Allemand*, the German and Austrian branch of the anti-Nazi resistance movement in France, organized by the French Communists and known as *Main d'Oeuvre lmmigrée* (September 1942 to June 1944). The third stage is with the *maquis*[2] in a French guerrilla unit that fought the Germans from its base in the hills southwest of Lyon and liberated the town of Tournon (July 1944–September 1944). The author and one of his friends were the only Austrians in that *maquis*. The fourth stage, after the liberation of France, refers to a small Austrian Volunteer Unit that made its way from France to Yugoslavia in an effort to join the Red Army's fight for the liberation of Austria (December 1944 to April 1945). The memoir ends in liberated Vienna, thus completing a full circle from Vienna 1938 to Vienna 1945.

THE REFUGEE

Until his arrival in Merxplas, the displaced persons' center in Belgium, Dolly Steindling was just another refugee. His crossing of the Swiss border, his passage to France, his stay in Paris and his entering Belgium — all this without the possession of any visa or even a passport — were experiences shared by many others. Refugee life, particularly in Paris, served as a literary motif in contemporary *belles lettres*, like Erich Maria Remarque's *The Arch of Triumph*.[3] In our author's tale we find in addition some important information on the work of the Jewish welfare organizations, as encountered by this young refugee. This evidence is expanded by his account of Merxplas, a refugee camp near Brussels established and maintained by the Jewish community in accord with the demand of the Belgian authorities to diminish the number of refugees who were living freely

Introduction

in the Belgian capital. It is at Merxplas that a turning point occurs in his life — and in his story. He ceases to be an individual refugee, becoming rather a member of a larger "family" — a group of young Austrian Communists and Socialists, well organized and run by able leaders. Dolly Steindling's earlier Socialist convictions and sensibilities were awakened there and shaped his life during the Holocaust era and for several decades later.

The comradeship and spirit of constant entrepreneurship made the inhuman conditions in the French camps Saint Cyprien and Gurs bearable. Gurs, where the author spent a year and a half from the fall of 1940 to the spring of 1942, has already been the subject of memoirs and scholarly works. Most of them focus on the catastrophic sanitary conditions, the hunger, and the resulting daily death toll. All this has been immortalized in a large number of drawings by artists who had been interned in Gurs; these drawings were given as a sign of gratitude to Elsbeth Kasser, the nurse who initiated and directed the humanitarian work of *Secours Suisse* in the camp.[4] Her involvement, as well as that of workers from other agencies, is also described in Dolly Steindling's testimony. As a consequence of the services that his group undertook and conducted, we find in his story a brighter aspect of life in the camp: the hopes and loves of young people that flourished in the midst of suffering, decay and despair.

In the spring of 1942 he and other members of the Austrian group were taken from the camp to a farm in a remote rural location in the southeastern part of France, where they were allowed to work under conditions of "assigned residence." But the onslaught on foreign Jews and their deportation "to the east," which the

Hitting Back

Vichy government unleashed in August 1942, were soon applied also to them. Their success in avoiding arrest and escaping the French police turned the author and his comrades into *illegal* refugees; their resolution to face the enemy and join the underground fight against the Germans transformed them into *combatants*.

TRAVAIL ANTI-ALLEMAND

According to Otto Niebergall, a leader of the German Communist party who was in exile in France, he together with leaders of the Austrian and Czech Communist parties, suggested to the Politburo of the French party sometime in 1941 that a special resistance organization be established to include German-speaking foreigners.[5] Their proposal was accepted and after further deliberations the specific purposes of the new unit were defined. The *Travail Anti-Allemand* (commonly known as *Travail Allemand* or T.A.) was to disseminate oral and printed anti-Fascist propaganda aimed at Wehrmacht soldiers, to locate and organize the anti-Nazi elements among them, to penetrate German occupation units, and to do whatever possible to undermine the German war effort. Until 1943 the operation was conducted by a single combined command. In that year the leadership of the German and Austrian underground was nominally separated. "This necessity resulted from the national question of Austria and Germany," emphasized Niebergall, alluding to the fact that the Allies recognized Austria that year as the first victim of German aggression. This decision, adopted at a meeting of the Allied foreign ministers in the second half of October 1943, had an immediate impact on the scope of activities of the anti-Nazis in Austria proper.[6] Its influence on the activities in France was of lesser

Introduction

importance and even the separation of the higher command did not affect the routine of close coordination. The organization in Lyon, the center of the T.A.'s operations in southern France, and in which Dolly was active at that time, was run by two leaders of the German Communist party and by Oskar Grossman, a leader of the Austrian party. Our author was in close contact with the latter early in 1944.

The story of the Austrian *Travail Allemand* has been told mainly by one person, Tilly Spiegel. Her research, published in 1969,[7] remains the dominant source of information, also for the volume on Austrians in exile, which appeared in 1984 as part of a comprehensive research project sponsored by the Austrian Federal Ministry of Science and Research. The introduction to the Ministry's volume states that "France, and first and foremost Paris, was, after the annexation of Austria, the center of the Austrian emigration." It also describes the whole spectrum of Austrian intellectual and political life that was transplanted to France after March 1938. The concise historical review on the Austrian resistance in France draws heavily on Tilly Spiegel's work.[8] Her account was based both on her own experience and other documentary sources. Tilly Spiegel was the liaison agent for Dolly Steindling, and for all the other members of the network in the Canal Zone region of northern France. She was his first contact after he managed to penetrate, as an employee, a German company that was building a section of Hitler's "Atlantic Wall." He was sent there by Franz Marek — later to become Tilly's husband — who was in charge of the T.A. in Paris and occupied France in late 1942.

The effort to convince German soldiers to turn against their own army, undertaken by male but mostly female members of the T.A., was extremely dangerous. Poorly printed and even handwritten periodicals and pamphlets were slipped into the hands of individual Wehrmacht personnel, who had been fraternized and seemed sympathetic to the anti-Nazi cause. For closer contact with possible recipients of such propaganda, efforts were made to find jobs as civil workers in the German army or other German units and organizations stationed in France. The Germans' need to maintain daily contact with the French created a demand for interpreters and individuals who could speak French fluently. Not easy to find among Germans, when French civilians who spoke German well were found they were used and later even trusted. This proximity with the enemy brought further advantages, like access to security stationery and seals and sometimes even to classified documents. A knowledge of French and German, exceptional audacity, and the ability to disguise oneself were essential conditions for success in this uneven struggle.[9] Tilly Spiegel's research shows that only a handful of young Austrians in France possessed these characteristics. She mentions only twenty-one girls who were active in the cities, and thirteen male and female combatants who were "incorporated" in (that is, had penetrated) German positions. Another seven individuals served as regional liaison agents with the central A.T. as well as with the local French *Résistance*, including Tilly herself.[10] These modest numbers are of course not conclusive, and further research might yield additional information; but being mainly concerned with individual cases, Tilly Spiegel's research must be considered at least indicative of the quantitative scope of that activity. Dolly Steindling was one of those few.

A notable role in the history of the Austrian resis-

Introduction

tance in France is played by the *Interbrigadiere*, the Austrian volunteers in the International Brigades who went to Spain to defend the legitimate Republican government after the civil war broke out in 1936. The persecution of the Communists and Socialists after their failed uprising in Austria in February 1934 led to a special relationship between Austrian left-wing partisans and Republican Spain. Their role during the Spanish Civil War and their fate after the Republic's defeat by Franco have been described in several memoirs and testimonies.[11] The military experience that the *Interbrigadiere* acquired in Spain, their training in clandestine activity, and their relationship with Spanish republicans in France — which was reinforced during their common internment in Saint Cyprien, Gurs, and other French camps — provided them with both the necessary know-how and the contacts for their work in the *Résistance*. They appear time and again in Dolly Steindling's story. His contacts with them in Lyon led to the next phase of his fight against the Nazis.

THE MAQUIS

Urban guerrilla warfare was the most common mode of fighting the German occupation until the summer of 1944. After Germany had occupied the rest of France in November 1942, rural guerrilla units, *maquis*, based mostly in mountainous areas, were strengthened by new recruits, usually young people who chose to fight the Germans over being forcefully enlisted by them to work in the "Great Reich." But it was not until summer 1944, particularly after the successful landing of the Allies in Normandy, that partisan warfare could play a vital role. The retreating German army, in addition to being routed by advancing Free French armies and the

Hitting Back

Allies after their disembarkment in southern France on 15 August, now also faced humiliating defeats by small, inadequately equipped and poorly organized local *maquisards* who descended upon them from their hideouts in the mountains. These guerrilla units, however, suffered heavy losses once the Wehrmacht began to launch counterattacks. It was at this time, summer 1944, after the T.A. in Lyon was decimated by a heavy blow inflicted by the Gestapo, that Dolly Steindling set out to join the French *maquis*.

His testimony provides an insight into a microcosm of events and human relations that in many cases accompanied and shaped the liberation of France. The conditions and routine at the guerrilla base in the bush; the attack on the German garrison at Tournon and the temporary success, defeat, and losses following the German return to the town; the ultimate liberation and subsequent outbursts of vengeance; and the dynamics of unlimited power bestowed, at least temporarily, on a low-ranking guerilla commander — all these features of the story are by no means of local significance only. For our author this was the first time he learned and actually used arms in combat. It was also the first time he was the "German" in a French unit. Accused of being German traitors, he and his friend — the only other Austrian — faced a "court martial" and barely escaped execution. That too was not a unique or extraordinary experience. At another *maquis* unit, this one a Jewish scouts' guerrilla unit named *Compagnie Marc Haguenau* after one of its victimized leaders, a large German armored force surprised the fighters at the very moment that Allied planes were parachuting arms, provisions, and personnel to them. Six of the fighters were killed and the suspicion of treason fell on one of the three

Introduction

German deserters who had joined the *maquis* some time earlier. Thanks to the integrity of the commander Robert Gamzon ("Castor") and his thorough investigation, the life of Hans, the German true anti-Nazi, was saved.[12] The ultimate successful culmination of the T.A.'s objectives — namely, motivating German soldiers to join the armed anti-Nazi resistance — led to a paradoxical and near-tragic outcome in the two episodes described here. Evidently, these were not the only episodes of this kind that occurred at that time in France. The author's experience helps us see them from the victim's perspective.

AN AUSTRIAN VOLUNTEER IN YUGOSLAVIA

During the second half of World War II, Slovenia, the northwestern province of what was the Monarchy of Yugoslavia, harbored strong partisan units that belonged to the Communist resistance movement headed by Josip Broz Tito. When the border between Austria and Yugoslavia was determined after World War I, it included many Slovenians in the Austrian province of Carinthia. Together with other Austrians, mostly Communists but also some active Catholics, they formed partisan units in 1944 under the supreme command of Tito. Heinrich Himmler, in his effort to suppress the resistance in 1944, was said to have called Carinthia a gang-infested area. The leaders of the Austrian Communist party arrived at Tito's headquarters from their exile in Russia and, with the dramatic advance of the Soviet Army towards Austria, Yugoslavia became the springboard for both the military liberation of Austria and the drive of the Austrian Communist party to secure its share in the liberated country.[13]

It was against this backdrop that the Yugoslav representative in Marseille agreed to make possible the transfer of the small group, to which Dolly Steindling belonged, from France via Italy to Belgrade. Small groups of Austrians, recruited in Yugoslavia from among countrymen who had escaped to areas held by the partisans, were incorporated into Austrian battalions. According to the testimony of a member of another group, by the time Austria was liberated, five such battalions reached Austria together with the Red Army. That source further states that the British intermediaries who organized the transport were not without a political agenda: they asked the group (of which that writer was a member) while it was in Italy on its way to Belgrade to join the right-wing monarchist resistance organization headed by General Draza Mihajlovic, which of course it refused.[14]

Dolly Steindling did not share this experience. However, his testimony suggests the utter marginality of the Austrians' pathetic endeavors to participate in the liberation of their country from their position in Yugoslavia.

THE JEWISH ASPECTS

"Jewish historiography has completely neglected Austrian-Jewish resistance," writes Arnold Paucker who researched the history of Jewish resistance in Germany.[15] This is partly connected to the denial of a singularly Jewish significance in the Austrian resistance. Tilly Spiegel, herself Jewish, was very explicit in this regard. In her letter to Yad Vashem in Jerusalem, together with extensive information that she provided about Jewish members of the Austrian Communist underground, she wrote:

Introduction

> I request that in any use for publication of the names and data which I have put at your disposal, the following historical truth should be respected: the mentioned Jewish Austrians in the French *Résistance*, both victims and survivors, fought because of their political or patriotic Austrian convictions. They were Jews, but they took part in the Résistance movement against Hitler's dominion as Austrians or as Austrian Communists. Indeed, Jews had the additional burning feeling of pain that their own parents, relatives and friends were innocently exposed to a horrible destruction when they could not save themselves through exile. But the Jewish comrades mentioned by me did not fight because of these feelings but out of their political enlistment, and so they also died. Conscience and morality oblige us to respect this fact.[16]

This emphatic assertion was completely in line with the way some Jewish members of the French *Résistance* felt about their activity. In October 1984 the *Association pour la Recherche sur l'Histoire Contemporaine des Juifs* (RHICOH, Association for Research of the Contemporary History of the Jews), that was founded to discover and make public the role that Jews had played in the French *Résistance*, organized a colloquium on "The Participation of Jews in the Liberation of the National Territory." They were utterly disillusioned to hear from some of the leading figures among the Jewish resistors quite the opposite of what they expected. "As far as I am concerned I am a Jewish Frenchman who resisted among other Frenchmen; I was not part of a Jewish *Résistance*, I was part of the French *Résistance*..." said Leo Hamon, an exceptional leader in de Gaulle's *Résistance* movement. "My resistance was not specifically Jewish," claimed Daniel Mayer, one of those who clandestinely reorganized the Socialist party as a resistance movement and who held senior ministerial positions after the war. Marc Bloch, the renowned historian of medieval France and among the first resistors, who was caught by the Germans, tortured and executed in 1944, wrote in his will in 1941: "I was born Jewish ... [but] estranged of all confessional formalism as well as of any pretended racial solidarity, I felt during my whole life, before anything and most simply, a Frenchman .... I die as I have lived — a good Frenchman." These notable Jews in the French *Résistance* acknowledged only that they were Jewish, denying any relationship between their Jewishness and what they had done as resistors.[17]

Are these sincere yet subjective assertions the only criterion by which their deeds should be judged?

Some historians accept them, believing it the exclusive right of the people involved to categorize the historical meaning of their own activities. Lucien Steinberg agreed that "it would be absurd to separate the various combatants of the *Résistance*, in other words, to create a ghetto there."[18] Others, like Renée Poznanski and André Kaspi, searched the "specific Jewish *Résistance*" in a functional differentiation between Jewish and general resistance. "In order to discover a truly Jewish resistance, one has to follow the activities of the Jewish organizations," says Kaspi in outlining the areas that require additional research on the history of the Jews in France during World War II.[19] This approach is best represented in the title of Lucien Lazare's work, *Rescue as Resistance, How Jewish Organizations Fought the Holocaust in France*. However, these two approaches do not cover very important segments of the French *Résistance* that were undeniably Jewish. First and foremost among them were the Jews in various M.O.I. (*Main d'Oeuvre Immigrée* "Immigrant Manpower") units, including

Introduction

exclusively Jewish units that were set up by the French Communist party. Jews were among the first and most violent urban guerrillas in Paris, regarding their enlistment primarily for the cause of communism, and also as French citizens (although many had obtained that citizenship only a short time before the war, many others were officially still foreigners). Lazare included the Jewish units of the M.O.I. among the Jewish armed resistors, but their extremely daring and risky operations did not include targets connected directly to the Holocaust, like trains on their way to Auschwitz, etc.[20]

Therefore, a more comprehensive approach to the Jewish resistance in France as well as elsewhere should be adopted. A considerable amount of evidence indicates that it is connected with the objective situation in which resistors, who were Jewish, found themselves because they were Jews.

Some of the testimonies quoted above provide a clue. Tilly Spiegel, despite her denial of any Jewish motive in the recruitment of Austrian Jewish resistors, recognized their consciousness of their own and their relatives' Jewish condition. Leo Hamon explained that the exclusively French character of his fight was a reaction to the enemy's determination to exclude Jews from the French nation. He elaborates, "...to people who wanted us to be nothing else but Jews, we responded that we were Frenchmen who were fighting them." Many Jews of all origins in France and elsewhere must have shared these feelings, since the phenomenon of a quantitative and qualitative disproportion of Jewish presence in the French clandestine organizations is a well-established fact. Henri Michel, a prominent French historian on France during World War II, wrote that "The participation of Jews in the *Résistance* was the highest, proportional to the population of Jewish religion or origin, of all the components of the *Résistance*, considered in their religious or ethnic aspects."[21] Maurice Kriegel-Vairimont who, before the war, was a Communist trade union leader and one of the participants in the 1984 debate, was one of the three members of the supreme committee that coordinated and commanded the *Forces Françaises de l'Intérieur* (the combined combat forces of the *Résistance*) just prior to and during the liberation of France. Another Jew — "Pierre Villon," born Roger Guinsburger — served with him on that committee. Several other leading resistors in a variety of organizations are also mentioned in Kriegel-Valrimont's short exposé, and Daniel Mayer as well as other participants added more names. Clearly, Jews played an especially prominent role — among the leadership as well as the rank and file — of the Communist resistance.[22]

Their particular condition as Jews must have encouraged a considerable number of them to join the *Résistance* and to excel already during the "black years" 1941–1943, when others found it difficult to detach themselves from their normal everyday life. That particularity continued to influence them even in the underground. True, unlike resistance organizations in Eastern Europe, anti-Semitism was not a factor in the French clandestine movements. Yet, Henri Noguères, a prominent Socialist and non-Jewish *Résistance* veteran, emphasized in the 1984 debate the lack of any difference between his Jewish and non-Jewish comrades, admitting that from time to time that difference occurred to him when he thought about the "additional danger" that his Jewish comrades faced. "It was at the moment of their arrest that we remembered that Marc Bloch, Benjamin Crémieux, and Jean Guy Bernard were Jewish.

Introduction

We became aware then of the particular gravity of the danger to which they were exposed."[23] Certainly the Jewish members of the *Résistance* were aware of the danger: they all changed their names and identity since their safety and very survival depended on their ability to disguise themselves as non-Jews. Furthermore, they had to hide their Jewish origin not only from the enemy but also from their oppressed fellow citizens. Aware that the German and Vichy propaganda depicted the whole *Résistance* as a purely Jewish-Bolshevik machination, exposure of their origin was considered a risk to the war effort of the Free French and the *Résistance*.[24]

Many Jewish resistors did not object to these conditions since they identified completely with the cause of the *Résistance*. They regarded their incorporation into the French *Résistance* as the achievement of a most cherished goal: the full acceptance of them as Frenchmen. After the war many retained their *nom de guerre*, while not denying their Jewish origin. Nonetheless this does not refute the objective fact that they were among the seventeen million Jews against whom Nazism and its followers in other nations waged a war of systematic discrimination and ultimate extermination. Whether they knew it or not, that war against the Jews contributed to their militancy and resistance and marked their particularity even among their comrades. Their resistance was thus, at least partly, an expression of the Jewish people's reaction against their aggressors.

"Socialist, then French and then a Jew," so Daniel Mayer defined the sequence of his identity and actions.[25]

In an almost identical way, Dolly Steindling defined himself at the time of his activity in France: Communist, Austrian, and then Jewish. Yet, the Nazi assault on the Jewish people was also the starting point on his itinerary as resistor. He never tried to deny that third element of his self-perceived identity, but it became the dominant factor when he was caught by the Gestapo. It appears though that his Jewishness came to the fore not only when he was threatened; it was also a positive assertion. Why else would he, an Austrian and a Communist disguised as a Frenchman lying in a hospital bed recovering from a gunshot wound, confide to a Catholic priest that because he was Jewish he could not repeat a Christian prayer? (p. 179). Nonetheless, he surely would have subscribed to Tilly Spiegel's request that historians present his and his comrades' fight as motivated by being Communist and Austrian but he would have omitted the exclusiveness of this demand.

Maurice Kriegel-Valrimont, the Jewish leader of the French Communist resistance, agreed in the 1984 debate that in view of a renewed wave of anti-Semitism and Holocaust denial that became evident at that time in France, the role of Jews in the *Résistance* should be singled out. Dolly Steindling would have agreed wholeheartedly with him. He too was alarmed by Fascist and neo-Nazi events that hit the headlines when he was writing his personal memoirs, and he commented on them in the margin of his annotations.

It is in this spirit of recognition of the Jewish aspect of his story that we present his work to the English-reading public.

Haim Avni

Note:

Italics are used in the author's text to emphasize certain words. In longer passages, italics indicate the author's reflections at the time of his writing.

REFUGEE

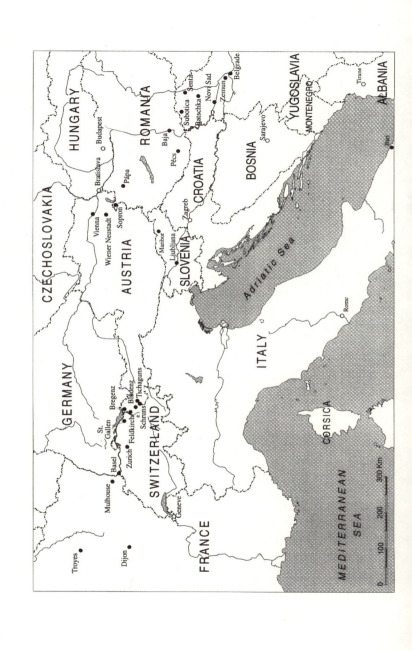

Vienna, The Anschluss, Departure

I was born October 15, 1918 in Wiener Neustadt, some 40 km south of Vienna in Austria. World War I was as good as over. The newborn baby knew nothing yet of the collapse of the Habsburg empire, the old emperor, the new republic, nationalism, religion or anti-Semitism; nothing of industry or money. Born into such an uncertain future, this innocent child was given a name — "Dolly." Papa was a non-commissioned officer in the army; he worked in the accounts department and was stationed at Wiener Neustadt. Mama looked after my elder brother Irving, known in the family as "Tutti." He was born in Berlin in that fateful year 1914. My parents, both born in 1889, originally came from Tarnow in Poland.

At the beginning of 1920 we moved from Wiener Neustadt to Vienna, more precisely to a modest, ground-floor apartment at 12 Schultz-Strassnitzky Street in the Alsergrund district of Vienna. There my sister Charlotte (Lotte) was born in 1921. We were now a family of six — Papa, Mama, Irving, myself, Lotte, and our maid — living together in a few small rooms. The hall was our playroom. Off the hall to the left was a kitchen living room, which, each evening and with the help of a folding bed, was turned into a bedroom for our maid. To the right of the hall was Irving's and my small bedroom. From the hall we could also reach the toilet. It was the type that flushed and was actually inside the apartment. This I considered particularly luxurious. We also had a bathtub in the kitchen. Having one's own toilet and bathtub indicated a certain degree of wealth; most

Hitting Back

houses in those days had only a shared toilet and tap in the hallway for use by the entire floor. Fate treated us well. Our bedroom window and the French terrace doors led on to a small courtyard overlooked by two windows of our neighbor's apartment. By climbing a small wall we could reach the backyard of a house in Röger Street — an ideal escape route for us when we had caused some trouble at home.

No day passed without street musicians performing outside the house. These were people without work who hoped to earn something by entertaining the residents. We sat on the windowsill with our legs dangling and sang along with the musicians whose performances often lasted all day. During this time of high unemployment many of them were disabled veterans from the First World War. They begged for something to eat, a few coins or just cigarettes.

After World War I my parents opened a grocery store on the corner of See Street and Rossauer Lände, which was only a short walk from the apartment. The Rossauer Lände, previously called the Empress Elisabeth Promenade, was known to us as the 'Promsch', a narrow park bordering the Danube canal. The shop, selling everything from fruit and vegetables to milk and cheese, was open from 6 A.M. until 7 P.M. and on Saturdays until 8 P.M. The brunt of the work both in the shop and at home with the family was borne by Mama. We always had enough to eat. Compared to most people at the time we were indeed fortunate. On the other hand we never had any cash to pay our rent (20 schillings a month), buy goods, or pay accounts. I remember how ashamed I was when my mother would send me to competitors to buy a few pounds of sugar, flour or some other item so that our customers would not notice that

Refugee

*Father (seated) and uncle,
World War I officers in the Imperial Austrian army*

we had nothing in stock. My parents ran the store until the Nazis marched into Austria in 1938. By 1939 the whole family had succeeded in leaving Vienna. As I begin to write now, it occurs to me that despite the desperate situation created by Hitler's invasion, we never discussed what we should do, or whether and how we should prepare our emigration. We simply left.

Hitting Back

But where to? This was the crucial question, discussed even among acquaintances who had seen each other only rarely in the past. There hardly existed a country that was not considered a potential refuge. Each country's immigration quotas for Austrians of all ages and professions were as well known to us as currency exchange rates are for bankers today. The possibilities of emigrating to Honduras, Nicaragua, Uruguay, Paraguay, Bolivia, Chile or British Guyana were discussed in great detail.

What we would do once we got there none of us knew. We vaguely imagined clearing land in small or large groups and forming agricultural communes. My ideal vision was to be a woodchopper in Canada. But Panama, The Dominican Republic, and Colombia were far more realistic possibilities. For all these countries there were of course certain prerequisites: the possession of a valid passport, an emigration permit, tax permits, and a visa. Then too the eternal maxim was true: you could acquire the necessary documents quickly if you had the money. For Brazil, Argentina and Venezuela you needed a considerable amount of money or, in its place, adequate business or private connections. The United States of course was the most desired destination. The magic word was *eiwideiwit* (affidavit), which meant that an American citizen had made a declaration to the authorities that the immigrant in question would not be a burden on the United States. With such a document and a place in the immigration quota, one's immigration into the United States was guaranteed, provided of course that one had the necessary emigration papers.

But the cardinal requirement for any of this was to stay alive. Every day, every hour was valuable. You never

Refugee

knew if you would survive the day or end up in prison or a concentration camp within a few hours. We still did not know what our destination would be. I had little chance of obtaining a visa, even less so the necessary emigration papers. The family had no money. Moreover, I knew myself — I would not have accepted abuse from the Nazis either towards my family or myself. My notorious short temper was an additional danger for us all.

The family

Hitting Back

Just five months after I left Vienna was "the night of the long knives." In one night, *Kristallnacht* (November 9–10, 1938), the Nazis slaughtered thousands of Jews, mainly in Vienna but also in Germany. They set fire to synagogues, Jewish businesses and schools.[1]

Neighbors, customers, former school friends, people with whom we had had daily contact for years, suddenly appeared in SA uniforms, wore swastikas, and played at being the "master race." Insults and assaults on Jews became commonplace. Plundering and robbery were daily events. Members of the so-called better circles of society "aryanized" Jewish businesses; "Aryanization" was officially approved confiscation whereby "evil" Jewish property became "good" Aryan assets. The call was already out: "Do not buy from Jews," "Do not employ Jews," "Do not work for Jews." The era of "race" had begun, starting with the introduction and enforcement of race violation laws.

Despite all this, at the beginning of May 1938 the rabid Nazis were still a minority. Many people in our immediate neighborhood behaved decently although it became increasingly difficult to maintain this publicly. No one knew what still awaited us; everyone knew that nothing good could be expected. Predictions for the future were as varied as the people who emitted them. People reacted very differently, according to their social position, origin, understanding, political opinion, religious belief and temperament. Our business went from bad to worse. Some of our Jewish customers had already left, and few non-Jews entered the store. Irving and I were without work or income. Each one of us turned every Schilling over five times before spending it. In very real terms we lived from the substance of our grocery shop. Our family had not yet really begun to suffer.

Refugee

It was against this background that I decided to flee Austria (then called "Ostmark") and, despite my scruples, leave my family. I was nineteen and a half years old. Today it is not uncommon for people of that age to have traveled widely. But I had been nowhere. Apart from visiting my grandparents in Poland as a child, I had never been further than Styria, knew nothing of the world, and knew nobody with whom I could have stayed. I only knew I had to get away from Vienna and away from the Nazis. Everything else was undecided and would be left to chance. Besides my temperament, my resolve was certainly also influenced by other factors. Social problems have always occupied and moved me: as a youth I had been a member of the Red Falcons (*Rote Falken*), the Socialist youth organization, and later of the Socialist Workers' Youth Organization (*Sozialistische Arbeiterjugend*), even at a time when this organization was illegal. At the same time I was a member of the Jewish youth organization *Hashomer,* which was also politically left of center.[2] Since the advent of Hitler in Germany, Mussolini in Italy, the civil war in Spain and the events in Austria between 1934 and 1938, the words 'Fascism' and 'democracy' were no longer abstract concepts for me. I knew that democrats and anti-Fascists, irrespective of whether they were agnostic or belonged to a religious community, were being imprisoned, interned in concentration camps, and often executed.

Conversations with friends had informed me that there were professional smugglers who would smuggle anyone for between 100 and 300 Reichsmark over the border. I discussed the possibility with two friends, Dolfi and Uli Engelstein. Uli was my age, Dolfi was three years older. Despite the age difference I was closer to Dolfi and we both wanted to go to Switzerland. Dolfi

Hitting Back

and Uli had an uncle in Zurich with whom they could expect to stay. Another two brothers, the Bielers, from our outer circle of friends would be joining us. I told my parents nothing of my plans. As it was, Mama was anxious and fearful — for the family and the future — and knowledge of my plans would only have caused tears. Papa was easily excitable and it seemed unlikely that rational, objective or even purposeful discussions could have taken place. I had already told Mama that I would need money for immigration and emigration documents. The family could not afford the sum of RM 150, but Mama had laid a little money aside and even asked two regular customers if they would be willing to help. Just before I was to leave, one of my aunts made up for the missing balance. The day of my departure came. I was to be the first to leave my family, parents, brother and sister, and enter the unknown. It was the beginning of May 1938. I had arranged with my friends that we would catch a train from Vienna's West Station late Saturday evening to Bregenz and from there attempt to cross the border.

On Saturdays our shop stayed open until 8 P.M. As always I helped in the shop but that afternoon I went home early to pack. My luggage consisted of a briefcase with necessary toiletries, a towel and underwear. When the whole family was at home just after eight o'clock, I told them that I would be leaving in a few minutes, what my plans were, and whom I was going with. Mama, Papa, Irving, Lotte and my aunt accompanied me to the Friedensbrücke — "The Bridge of Peace." There we parted tearfully. I traveled by tram to the West Station.

Before boarding the train I discovered that there would not be five but six of us. Without previously informing us, the Bieler brothers had brought an

Refugee

The shop
Dolly (on the right), Mama, sister, and brother

acquaintance whom we didn't know. I have forgotten his name but will call him "Gabor." The train journey went without incident. When we got to Bregenz, Dolfi searched out the man who would smuggle us over the border and brought him to a coffeehouse where we were waiting. We agreed on a price of 100 Reichsmarks per head for the crossing. He would guide us over the Silvretta mountains to Swiss territory, from where we would descend to St. Gallen. We traveled with him — although in separate compartments of the train — to Schruns and further, higher to Tschaguns in the Vorarlbergian Montafon region. He led us to a mountain hut where we ate supper, and told us to get some rest as we

Hitting Back

had to leave after midnight. He collected the 100 marks agreed upon from each of us and left, telling us that he had to fetch maps. We never saw him again. Shortly after he left, a group of gendarmes arrived and arrested us. After taking our money he had reported us.

The gendarmes took us back to Schruns where they locked us up in the police jail, and notified the Gestapo in Feldkirch. Two days later we were collected by the Gestapo and moved to Feldkirch. The interrogations were not particularly dramatic. We had to explain exactly why we had come to Tschaguns, as the Gestapo were attempting to discover whether we were politically active or were trying to get to Spain in order to join the International Brigades. After two days of questioning we were moved to the regional prison of Bludenz. This was how I came to know the beautiful province of Vorarlberg. We remained in solitary confinement. No one would tell us what would happen or how long we would be held. It soon became clear that the "friendly" guide was working with the Gestapo, as his name was systematically ignored during the questioning. It enraged us that he would continue to cash in on other unfortunate refugees before delivering them to the police. The interrogation was repeated again and again. Everything we had told the police and the Gestapo was documented several more times. The offices in Vienna also became involved in the investigations, but we were small fry and none of us had a previous record.

Soon after our imprisonment I got into conversation with our warder and his wife. I explained our plight and told him that all we wanted was to reach safety over the border in a neighboring country. He had previously been a Social Democrat and was afraid he would lose his position, but he allowed me to work in the prison kitchen

Refugee

and clean windows. In exchange, his wife cooked *Buchteln* for me, a sort of Austrian unsugared doughnut in vanilla sauce. After several days, upon my request, we were transferred to a larger common cell and were allowed to walk in the prison courtyard. The warder told us that even if the smuggler had not betrayed us we would not have succeeded in escaping over the border because our clothing was totally unsuitable. I was wearing town shoes and a casual suit with long trousers, and my friends were dressed much the same. At that time of the year, snow lay at least knee deep in the mountains. We had neither the equipment nor the mountaineering experience necessary for the task at hand. But we were indeed fortunate that the warder was such a decent man — he explained exactly how and where we could cross into Switzerland.

After three weeks in prison Gabor and I were released. Each of us received discharge papers stating the length of our imprisonment and that nothing incriminating had been found against us. We followed the advice of the prison warder in Bludenz to the letter, and thanks to his suggestions we were able to leave "Ostmark" behind us. My four friends, the Engelstein and Bieler brothers, were released three weeks later and also managed to escape the Nazis and reach Switzerland.

The Road to Switzerland

Immediately after our release from prison we bought two waterproof bags that we could strap to our bodies with a belt. We made our way to Hohenems — knowing that a main road led from there into Switzerland — and would cross the border, which was the old bridge over the Rhine, into Dippoldsau, the village on the other side. Our first attempt to cross the border illegally had been unsuccessful, but Gabor and I were to have more luck with our second effort — despite our naiveté.

On the day of our release, at the beginning of June 1938, we reached Hohenems in the afternoon. We found the road leading to the Swiss border on our map and, carrying our small briefcases, marched alongside it. As I recall we hardly saw traffic or people. Nobody seemed to notice us and we registered that positively. After walking for about half an hour we were approached by two customs officers riding bicycles. We looked past them blankly. They stopped and asked us where we had come from and what we wanted here. I answered that we were from Vienna and were heading for Dippoldsau. One of the officers said that Dippoldsau was in Switzerland and asked to see our passports. "We don't have any," we replied in unison. They looked at each other and then at us in disbelief. Following a short discussion I presented our prison release papers and the evidence that we were neither criminals nor was there any charge against us. Since they were pleasant and seemed trustworthy, we told them that we were Jews and wanted to reach Switzerland because we could no longer live in "Ostmark." Again, luck was on our side. The two cus-

Refugee

toms officers proved to be both compassionate and honorable. Had they been simply congenial, as many people are, we would undoubtedly have run into the Swiss police who at that time handed over hundreds if not thousands of refugees to the German authorities. That in fact is how so many who were already on Swiss soil and believed themselves to be safe ended up in German prisons or concentration camps.

They advised us to hide until dusk and then to go to the customs house where they were on duty, promising to show us the way over the border. We had nothing to lose and felt we could trust them. When we arrived at the customs house late that evening they were already expecting us. The old dried-out riverbed of the Rhine, which was the border, was nearby. The route they advised was almost the same as that described by the prison warder in Bludenz. We waited until it was almost completely dark and at eleven o'clock we left. Both officers accompanied us as far as they could, about one kilometer along the old riverbed. We thanked them for their help and said goodbye. How fortunate for us to have crossed the path of such humane people. We took off our shoes, tying the laces together, and hung them around our necks. Slowly and with great care we made our way down the embankment, but still could not avoid pebbles moving as we crossed the stony riverbed and climbed up the opposite embankment. Swiss soil! At even the faintest noise we stopped and held our breath, not daring to move. Each rolling pebble seemed to cause the roar of an avalanche. We were sure the Swiss border guards must have heard us and we were terrified of their search dogs, about which we had been told. Each time we overcame our fear and took another hesitant and careful step. After eventually reaching the

Hitting Back

top rim of the embankment we lay on the ground totally still and listened for some sign that we had been noticed, gradually regaining our composure and catching our breath. With our shoes back on we walked through the fields parallel to the main road. St. Gallen was our goal but we would have to cross the Rhine to reach it. The customs officers had told us that we would see the bridge over the Rhine from a distance as it was well lit. The prison warder in Bludenz had warned us that although the bridge was situated deep in the Swiss country it would be guarded; we should avoid it and swim across the Rhine instead. This was the reason for our purchasing the waterproof bags. We had rolled up the legs of our trousers but our shoes and socks were already soaked through from walking in the fields. It did not take long until we saw the lights of the bridge. Distancing ourselves from the road we carefully approached the river. We undressed, packed only what we absolutely needed in the waterproof bags and threw the rest of our belongings into the river. Our hearts racing, we walked slowly into the Rhine. It must have been fear that drove us because we could barely move our limbs in the icy water. We had to swim against the flow that was taking us downstream, but we managed to reach the other bank. While drying off and trying to warm up we searched for new strength. Only then did we dare, softly, to talk to each other about the second stage of our journey — the route to St. Gallen.

Once we had found the way back to the main road we trudged at a safe distance from it through the fields towards St. Gallen. Our shoes were sodden through but we couldn't allow that to disturb us. Walking in the fields was difficult; the ground was uneven and we couldn't see the potholes. We stumbled often and our

Refugee

feet ached. I suggested that we aim for the main road, despite the dangers, so that we could proceed faster. Cautiously we approached the ditch at the side of the road, trying to get a view of both sides, left and right, before stepping onto it. At that moment a light went on in a house on the other side of the road. A window was opened on the upper floor and somebody leaned out. The window was closed again but the shadow of a human figure remained standing behind it. As soon as the light had gone on we dived behind a nearby bush. We were certain that we had been heard, perhaps even seen, and would soon be discovered. We were petrified. Only after the window had been closed did we dare to squat. Our knees began to shake, the muscles of our thighs stiffened with fear. We could still see the shadow behind the window. I persuaded Gabor that we had to go on and after some hesitation he followed me. Only then did we realize that it had been an optical illusion. What had appeared to us as the shadow of a man looking directly at us was in fact a suit hanging on the window frame! Greatly relieved but considerably shaken, we slowly and silently continued on our way, our pace increasing as our nerves calmed. Without further complications we reached the town of St. Gallen from where we took the seven o'clock morning train to Zurich.

From Zurich to France

We had scarcely taken a few steps from Zurich's main railway station when a man of about thirty addressed us, asking the way to the Jewish Community offices. He was Viennese and had assumed from our clothing that we were too. We could not help him but soon discovered that we had a common acquaintance. Antal's, the delicatessen at the corner of Strassnitzky and Rotenlöwen Street, was known to us both. "Mr. Antal is in Paris," he told me and I noted the address. This chance meeting was later to play a not-insignificant role.

Gabor and I finally arrived at Dolfi Engelstein's uncle's house in Badener Street. He took us in. The next day, rested and with a more civilized appearance, we went with him to the Jewish Community Center.[3] There we were given pocket money and cigarettes and told to register with the canton police of the fourth region. Forms were filled out and we left the police building with a provisional residence permit. A few days later, however, I got to know the canton police from a different angle.

Gabor and I found a cheap room in an attic and moved in immediately. During the next few days we began to find our way around Zurich. We were strictly forbidden to work and had to live from the support that the Jewish Community provided — 17 Swiss francs a week. Fortunately we could eat very cheaply at the Epa or Mika department stores. With papers stating that we received support from the Jewish Community, we could prove that we were not a burden on the Swiss state. To be noticed unfavorably in Switzerland could mean deportation to the German border.

Refugee

It was urgent that I contact my family in Vienna. A few days later I received various documents including my certificate of nationality. Like my parents, I was an Austrian citizen, a citizen of a country that no longer existed. Gabor's situation was more complicated. He had lived with his mother in Vienna for a long time, fifteen years, but he was not Austrian. He was Polish, although born in Hungary. The Poles no longer recognized the citizenship of Jews who did not live in Poland, and they refused to issue a document certifying this loss of citizenship. People like Gabor, therefore, did not have the right to be recognized as being "stateless" or to receive a "stateless" passport. Gabor was *nothing*. In order to own some form of document he was advised to apply for a document from the post office. The commissioner of the canton police who was working on our file promised to help.

We had been living in our room in the loft for a week when Gabor went off one morning to fetch his document from the post office. He never came back. Years later I heard from common friends that he had been deported by the Swiss to the German border, was taken to a concentration camp, and died there. But I did not know that then.

As Gabor did not return during that night or the next morning, I went to the canton police and registered him as a missing person. I received no answer, not even a look of surprise or sympathy. When I had finished explaining what had happened, the amiable commissioner told me to empty the contents of my pockets on the table. Then without any explanation he had me led away to prison where I was put into a solitary cell. I did not suffer from hunger and was even given hot chocolate to drink. I was not interrogated and I did not have

Hitting Back

to make a statement. Apart from the prison warder I saw no one. I had no inkling of what lay ahead and my worst fear was that I would be deported back to Germany.

I was given soap and a towel but no comb, razor or toothbrush. Several times a day, but without success, I demanded to see the authorities to find out why I was being held. I also insisted that the Jewish Community office be informed of my imprisonment. Finally, a week later, two police officers from the Department for Foreigners came to the prison to escort me to the Jewish Community Center. I was unshaven and looked thoroughly unkempt. The contents of my pockets were not returned to me. We went by foot over the Sihl Bridge and because of the heavy pedestrian traffic both policemen, who were not in uniform, walked two paces in front of me. At this point two other policemen stopped me and demanded my papers — not surprising considering my appearance. Only after the plainclothes policemen had identified themselves could we continue on our way. The Jewish Community vouched for me, so back we went to the canton police. There the contents of my pockets were returned to me, but I had to promise to leave Zurich as soon as possible.

About two weeks later I moved to Basel and there too I received a provisional residence permit. Again I was not allowed to work or earn money. I lived from the pocket money and cigarettes I was given by the Jewish Community Center. The number of emigrants was growing, many of them felt no shame in cadging and begging. It made me uneasy. The German border was nearby and there were stories of emigrants who had been picked up at night by the Swiss police and deported over the German border. I knew nobody in Basel and had no friend among the emigrants. I was entirely alone.

Refugee

Basel lies also on the French border. I had heard that France was willing to take a few political refugees each day. My thoughts turned in this direction. I had the Paris address of my cousin, S. H., in my notebook. That was all. I had no money for the journey and neither passport nor visa. How was I to get to Paris? My knowledge of French was extremely poor as I had studied it only once a week as a subsidiary subject in high school. Yet these considerations hardly occurred to me; my desire to be in safety and begin life anew somehow suppressed all else.

In retrospect, it is clear that at that time — and also later in my life — I often acted impulsively. Perhaps that is part of my temperament, but overall, I can say with certitude that I regret nothing.

After spending about ten days in Basel I left neutral Switzerland. My luggage still consisted of only one briefcase. At the end of June 1938 at three o'clock in the morning I illegally crossed the border near Basel into France and reported to the French border post in St. Louis. After minimal questioning I was granted a provisional residence permit for France, good for all provinces except Bas Rhin, Haut Rhin, Moselle, Seine, Seine et Marne, and Seine et Oise. Although the *département* Seine was Paris, and the other Seine provinces its outskirts, Paris was my destination. In spite of the regulations of my new host country, I had to get to Paris. I knew no one in the whole of France and all I had was the address of my Parisian cousin.

From St. Louis I travelled to the nearby town of Mulhouse, which was in the *département* Haut-Rhin, also forbidden in my residence permit. I located the Jewish Community Center and although they were not partic-

Hitting Back

ularly welcoming, they provided me with a railway ticket to Dijon and the address of the local rabbi. Once there I would decide how to continue. I traveled on the night train and arrived in Dijon in the early hours of morning. After spending some hours in the station waiting room I went to the address I had been given, hoping the rabbi would be able to help or at least advise me. I rang his bell first at nine o'clock, then again at ten. When I rang it for the third time at eleven o'clock that morning and there was still no response I was quite downhearted. I was also very hungry. Nearby a grocery store was selling three bananas for a franc. I bought ten, sat on the steps of the house and began to eat one banana after the other. My hunger dissipated but my worries remained. The landlady of a bistro on the other side of the street must have been watching me and she beckoned me to go over to her. I showed her the piece of paper with the name and address of the rabbi, and guessed more than understood her reply, that the family was away on vacation. We tried to communicate with a few words but mostly gesticulations. I told her I was a "fugitive" (the word *réfugié* I learned only later) from Vienna, in Austria. She quickly understood that I had no money, nothing to eat and nowhere to sleep. Two policemen who were sitting at the bar heard, or rather saw, our conversation and invited me for a *tartine beurrée*, boiled eggs and beer. Before they left they gave me the address of the police station and gave me to understand that if the worst came to the worst I could sleep there. Aimlessly and with no sense of time I wandered through the strange town. In the evening I rang the Rabbi's doorbell once again. Again there was no response so I went to the police station. There I was given something to eat and was allowed to spend the night. The

Refugee

next morning they presented me with money they had collected among themselves for a rail ticket to Troyes, in the *département* Aube. They truly embodied the maxim, "The police is your help and your friend."

I think that up until that point my morale was relatively high; the breakdown was still to come. I was to go to Troyes, a small town halfway between Dijon and Paris, although I had no reason to be there and knew no one. The only thing Troyes had in its favor was that it lay closer to my goal, Paris. But in Dijon I got on the wrong train. This I only discovered after traveling for a long time through a thinly populated area when the conductor checked my ticket and attempted to explain my error to me. I had to get off the train at the next station. The train back to Dijon with a connection to Troyes would only leave the next day. There I was, in an abandoned wooden hut they called a railway station, with not a house in sight. I walked along the ill-kept main road, passing fields and a forest, left the road and sat on a tree stump in despair. Everything knotted inside me. I was homesick, hungry and my feet ached. Lonely and miserable, I felt like an outcast. I cried all the tears I had inside me and ate the bananas and bread left in my case. I took out a pad and began to write a letter home expressing my sense of desolation and panic. I felt better. Wisely, I later tore up the letter; it would only have caused my family heartbreak. They had enough problems of their own. Still, committing the misery I felt to paper was cathartic. I had managed to bridge the hollow of my depression.

I returned to the station and spent the night in the waiting room. Except for the stationmaster I had seen nobody in this nest of a place. The following morning I returned to Dijon and took the correct train to Troyes.

Hitting Back

Now I was in Troyes — so what? I never intended to stay here, so I had to continue improvising my way to Paris. I walked through the streets of the town and at about midday stopped at a bistro for boiled eggs with bread and butter and a drink. My method of communication was again wild gesticulations because of my poor French. A destitute-looking character sitting at a table intervened, claiming to speak German. He was a Pole and I think his German was worse than my French but he managed to translate for me. There would be a market the following day and he would introduce me to some Jewish merchants. In the meantime I could stay with him. I had a sense of disquiet about it, but as I owned nothing that was worth stealing I went with him.

His room was utterly squalid and filthy. It soon became clear that he was a homosexual so I put on all my clothes again and lay on the floor. He left me in peace but sleep was out of the question. In the morning we went to the market together but I wanted to be rid of the fellow. While he was speaking to a trader I entered a toilet on the market square and when I saw that he was looking for me in the wrong direction I fled, asking my way until I reached the railway station. As I stood in the vicinity of the ticket office with no plan and no idea what to do next, I overheard two well-dressed gentlemen speaking German. I gathered up every bit of courage and approached them. They were from Alsace. After I had explained my predicament they gave me the money for a ticket to Paris.

Paris

Albeit without official permission I had finally managed to reach my destination. At this very time King George VI of England was visiting Paris. The security provisions were consequently very strict and several thousand "undesirable foreigners" had had to leave Paris — even Poles and other such immigrants who had been living there for ten years and more. Railway stations and public buildings were particularly well guarded. My mind was awhirl with curiosity, insecurity, hope, confidence, and, through it all, dread of the police. Everything was a muddle, but I was stubbornly determined to struggle on.

The address of my Parisian cousin was in my notebook. Knowing this gave me the sense that I was no longer alone. The train rolled into Gare de l'Est. Uniformed and plainclothes policemen were everywhere but I reached the exit of the station unhindered. There I literally flung myself into a taxi. After slamming the door behind me I breathed a sigh of relief, too soon though. "Hotel Akazia in rue Miami, please," I whispered. Although my strongest desire was to leave the station as quickly as possible the driver made no motion to leave but asked me again for the address, which I, becoming increasingly nervous, repeated. He shook his head vigorously, gave me to understand that he knew no rue Miami, and sought help in his street guide. I sat as if on glowing coals. The taxis behind us drove off one after the other and I had the impression that all the people standing by, including the policemen, were staring at the car in which I sat. After studying the street map thoroughly the driver told me with regret in his voice that there was no rue Miami in Paris. My heart was already beneath my stomach and could fall no further. I presumed that the problem lay in my abominable accent and lack of knowledge of the language. Then I remembered: the stranger who had spoken to us on the street in Zurich had given me the Paris address of our common acquaintance, Mr. Antal, which was written below my cousin's address — "Hotel des Acacias" on the Acacias Street. In order to avoid any further difficulties in communication, I passed the driver my address book and pointed to S. H.'s address to prove that rue Miami was correct. The driver beamed, put the car into gear, accelerated and drove off. While driving he half-turned towards me, gave me back my address book and said, "Ah, rue des Acacias!" In fact he said a great deal more that I did not understand. What was important was that we put distance between ourselves and the station. It was all the same to me whether we would land up first at S. H.'s in the rue Miami or at Mr. Antal's in the rue des Acacias. The taxi stopped in front of the Hotel des Acacia's in the rue des Acacias. Opposite was the Hotel Miami. (I should mention that Mr. Antal had stayed for a short time at the Hotel des Acacias but apparently he had moved out long ago. I never again heard anything of him.)

> *My objective in Paris, the meeting with S. H., does not merit a heading, not even in this autobiography of a non-author. Nevertheless, the meeting with him was not without repercussions for me. These were neither desired by him nor understood by me. In a word, S. H. was the quintessence of a man whose every action is driven solely by self-interest. Only later did I realize that he was merely one repre-*

sentative of a whole category of such people. At that time I was just beginning to develop an awareness for such things.

After I had paid the taxi I looked around and hesitantly entered the hotel. It was perhaps ten o'clock in the morning. I went up to the doorman and asked for S. H. He told me that Monsieur H. was still sleeping at this time. I thanked him and left my name with the message that I was a cousin from Vienna and would return in half an hour. I left the hotel and explored the area. The Hotel Miami was not large but it was a very elegant hotel in an expensive district of Paris near the Place de l'Etoile. S. H. was a diamond trader, just like his father, one of my mother's brothers. Mr. H. senior had built up the business in Berlin where they had lived until 1936, three and a half years after Hitler came to power. They left Germany that year and settled in Antwerp. S. H.'s elder brother ran a jewelry shop in New York.

Dolly Steindling in January 1939

Hitting Back

At around eleven o'clock I returned to the hotel. I was informed by the concierge that Monsieur H. was still sleeping but I could take a seat in the meantime. I sat in an armchair in the small lobby and waited. I didn't want to trouble the concierge a third time and I sat there for two hours. Although at the time ignorant of Einstein's theory of relativity, I understood that time could be both long and short. Those two hours were interminable. It was not until after 1 P.M. that the concierge came to tell me that Monsieur H. had been informed of my presence and had asked whether I would like to eat something. I had forgotten that I was hungry but when the porter asked me, my stomach answered immediately and I accepted. They would be honored to serve me.... A few minutes later I was brought a small sandwich and coffee. I had last eaten, and then only barely, at the railway station at Troyes but Mr. H. could not know that. I was to wait another hour and a half before I was to meet my cousin personally. Finally, a short, stout young man with reddish-blond hair walked towards me. He did not introduce himself and was obviously annoyed by the disturbance. It was more of a statement than a question when he said, "So you are Dolly!"

Our conversation — or rather his monologue — took place in the hotel lobby. Where else could he have taken me? His rooms had not yet been cleaned, Monsieur had just got up, finished his *petit déjeuner*, was now full, and perhaps also satisfied with the previous evening's entertainment or with the business transactions of the previous day. How should he cope with a cousin who has suddenly turned up in Paris in the early afternoon? If one hardly gets to bed before 4 o'clock in the morning, it is only natural to get up around noontime. This is wholly logical and I should not get the wrong impression. In addition *Monsieur* is a very busy man. To fly once, perhaps even twice, a week to Prague is very tiring. In Prague there are Jews and also non-Jews fleeing Hitler who often had jewelry but no money to finance their further flight. To buy up this jewelry cheap — pardon, to help these people — is a religious obligation, a *mitzvah*. He was acting out of charity.... What was not subsequently sold in Paris could still be profitably sold in New York or Antwerp. Of course, he himself occasionally had to travel to Belgium, which was also very strenuous. He spoke about himself with the utmost self-pity, and seemed almost in tears. Should I perhaps have wept with him? By then I had already completely forgotten my own existence.

Suddenly, *Monsieur* appeared to notice my presence and asked: "Where is my aunt? Where is the family?" "Unfortunately still in Vienna," I answered, "I am the first to get away." I was not allowed the opportunity to describe how and under what circumstances I had left Austria. His voice became cooler and harder as he asked the next question: "And why did you leave home? What are you doing here in Paris?" Until this point I had been merely bewildered, perhaps even fascinated like a child is by a magician's tricks. But this question and the tone in which it was posed evoked in me a feeling I did not know before. "Have you ever heard of Hitler and the Nazis?" I asked him. "And what has that got to do with it?" he replied. A distressing silence fell. I stared right through him. I was confronted with a being from another planet. He was from Germany, I from Austria. We spoke the same language but we could not comprehend each other. We were relatives, but we could not relate to each other. We were even less than strangers to each other. I was utterly disgusted, shaken and lost some of my illusions. Later on I would lose many more. I was a problem for him, and he had to rid himself of me. He found a way out: "Dolly, you must be tired. I will take you to a hotel." No sooner said than done. We walked to the Avenue de la Grande Armée that was not far. The hotel was near the Place de l'Etoile. He negotiated the price of a room for me, gave me the address of the Jewish Community Center and, with evident relief, said almost affably, "If you need anything, ring me up." He did not ask if I had enough money for the hotel room. Such trifles did not concern *Monsieur*. And with that he left. I would manage without Mr. H.

I did not see him again until 1940 in a camp at Saint Cyprien after Hitler had overrun Belgium and France. He was in the neighboring *îlot* (enclosure). When I was able to get hold of some food I would push it to him through the barbed wire. He would whimper like a dog. In those circumstances he wanted to rekindle our relationship, but for me he was a nonentity. He managed to escape from the camp by bribing guards with diamonds he had hidden on his body. Needless to say, he once again forgot he had a relative imprisoned in the same camp. He never changed....

The Refugee's Reality

I deposited my bag in my room, left the hotel and was ready to absorb the atmosphere of Paris. There was far more traffic than I had seen in any other city. I studied the map at a metro station with interest, saw the Arc de Triomphe in front of me and walked down the Champs Elysées. It was beautiful. The impressions were so overwhelming that I never even gave a thought to the fact that I was here illegally. Paris was a forbidden city for me. I knew that this metropolis with its outskirts had a population of about five million people, but the knowledge alone was of little help as I knew not one of them. I had forgotten S. already.

The next morning I visited the Jewish Community Center,[4] where masses of emigrants were already waiting. After a long wait I was given fifty francs as support and told that it was not possible to find a job; there were no work permits to be had and too many emigrants. Somebody advised me to go to the Austrian Committee on rue de Varenne. There I met people from Vienna, none of whom I knew. In the course of several conversations, however, I discovered that my friend Leo Weitz was in Paris, but no one knew his address. In rue de Varenne I was also given fifty francs. As grateful as I was, it was more important to me to have an address in this city of millions where I could meet my compatriots.

My hotel room cost eighty francs a week, so there was little left to live on. I immediately wrote home and asked my parents to send me Leo Weitz's address. His parents and elder brother were still in Vienna. Mama was delighted to have news of me. A few days later the answer came with Leo's address. Ten German Reichsmarks were enclosed in the letter. Knowing how Mama longed for news of me I bought blocks of ten postcards, wrote a few cards at a time and each day upon leaving the hotel dropped one in the mailbox. *The idea of calling on the telephone — today as simple as phoning next door — never occurred to me.*

I went to see Leo Weitz where I also met a common friend, Arthur D. from Vienna. The next day I moved into their hotel, the Mont Cenis on Boulevard de la Chapelle at the metro station Barbès-Rochechouart. The room cost thirty-five francs a week. When I say "at the metro station" I mean it literally — the metro ran almost through my room. The tracks there are not underground but built on cast-iron scaffolding so that with every train that passed all the houses around trembled. Neither this nor the run-down state of the narrow houses, which were nearly all hotels, nor the condition of the room, the beds or the stand-up toilet bothered me. Montmartre and above all Pigalle were nearby. There were street markets and there were whores. You could not walk past the hotels on the Boulevard de la Chapelle, including the Mont Cenis, without being approached by several of them at the same time. They seemed to be of all ages. There was no reason to be scared, particularly if you had nothing in your pockets. Because of the difficult times and the heavy competition the girls had to advertise their business as blatantly as possible. Most of the rooms in my hotel and those nearby were inhabited or used at times by these ladies of the night. There were times during my stay there when I had absolutely no money to buy food. Sometimes I lay on my bed during the day with the door half open because of the heat, and it was not uncommon for these

Refugee

friendly girls to provide me with both food and human warmth.

No work permits were being issued in Paris. Leo Weitz, Arthur D., and I had to look around for badly paid, illegal work. We performed our first joint job in our hotel room, assembling radio plugs. With a simple gadget we attached laminae to both ends of a carbon rod. Each of us had to produce a quota of a thousand pieces a day. The work went quickly but was indescribably tedious. What we earned barely covered our rent and food. After about fourteen days we had produced enough and the job was at an end. I then found work as a car washer. I didn't own rubber boots and none were put at my disposal, so I worked barefoot. After a few days my legs were so swollen that I had to give up the job. The next job I found was cleaning vegetables at the Restaurant Franco-Allemand on the Boulevard St. Denis. The working hours were from six in the morning to three in the afternoon. At about eleven o'clock I was given some foul slop, which I couldn't bring myself to swallow despite my hunger. When I asked for my pay after three days the owner replied that all I could expect was my food. On the fourth day I did not return.

In the meantime I had got to know several emigrants, Viennese, Germans and some Poles. But these connections were not very strong, particularly with the people from Vienna, as most of them were older than I. One of my friends from Vienna, a certain Popper, gave me the address of a common friend, Felix. His parents were wine wholesalers in Vienna. Through these connections he was allowed to work legally in Paris as a waiter in a first-class hotel in the rue de Rivoli. Leo Weitz and I often waited at the staff entrance and Felix would bring us wonderful food: ham, roast chicken, eggs, but-

Hitting Back

ter and fruit that had been returned to the kitchens untouched by the guests. For us those days were holy feasts.

Many emigrants lived from begging, or selling merchandise such as office equipment, cosmetics, clothing — according to lists of names and addresses they were given. But this was little more than thinly veiled begging. At the beginning it seemed a good idea, but one had to pester the potential buyers and with luck they paid you off with a little charity. Karli Nassau, who had been my best friend at school and until I left Vienna, was also in Paris and lived two hotels away on the Boulevard de la Chapelle. We were the same age but he was much bigger and far stronger than I. He was a swimmer and a boxer and in top physical condition. Somebody took him to work at the market halls and he passed the tip on to me. So I tried Les Halles, the central market, "Paris's stomach" — *le Ventre de Paris* — as the title of a novel by Emile Zola has it. At that time the market was in the center of the city. In the early hours of the morning when the goods arrived we tried to get allocated to the unloading of at least one truck; the pay was between ten and fifteen francs for each truck load. One had to be quick and strong. The advantage of this job was that we got the money immediately and the police turned a blind eye. I don't believe any of the laborers, whether from Poland, Morocco, Algeria, Tunisia, or Indochina, possessed a working permit. With my market experience from Vienna, I focused on the trucks containing crates of fruit as these were the least heavy. I was quick but compared to the strong and robust men there I had no chance. Now and then I managed to earn ten to twenty francs but it left me completely exhausted. Still, I could eat almost as much fruit as I wanted and even take some home.

Mama sent me the address of an engineer, a German emigrant who had lived and worked in Paris for some years. Perhaps he could help me. When I looked up the family he wasn't at home but his wife made me something to eat. I met him the second time I went and he seemed a calm and pleasant enough man, but how could he help me find work? I visited another two or three times, and at each visit his wife made me take care of household chores in exchange for her *taking care* of me.... I did not go back. I was lucky then to find work in my own profession (for which I had trained in Vienna) at a *chapelier* (hatter), where I earned fifty-five francs a week plus lunch. But unfortunately after a few weeks he had no more work for me. Once a month mama sent me ten marks, which certainly helped but I worried about whether they could spare it.

    I cannot remember how long I stayed with Leo Weitz in the Hotel Mont Cenis. It became increasingly difficult to stay in Paris without a residence permit. I moved to Chelles, an eastern suburb of Paris and only thirty minutes away by train, bus or metro. Living there was much cheaper than in the capital. Six of us shared an apartment consisting of two rooms and an alcove for cooking. With three of us in each room it was very tight. Many emigrants, including Viennese, lived in Chelles because of the harassment by police in Paris. At least in Chelles we were allowed to be registered, a fact that improved our situation enormously. Although my family had sent me clothes from Vienna, I did not have many and needed very few. Needless to say I did not look very elegant. Because I was skinny and looked younger than I was — I was twenty — I received an offer from a *keiler*. A *keiler* is a con-man who uses his gift of persuasion to sell overpriced goods that can be bought cheaper elsewhere. With me acting as his starving child he could make a quicker sale by working on the buyer's sympathy. I played this role for two weeks, earning more than I would have doing any manner of hard labor, but this deception didn't sit well with me. My benefactor could not understand it.

Where there are Viennese there is a coffeehouse. At the coffeehouse in Chelles I could usually earn some money. The head cook was a Viennese woman of about thirty-five, who coincidentally was also called Dolly. With my namesake from home in this foreign little town, I was in good hands.

Belgium

In Austria the situation was becoming increasingly serious. My brother managed to escape to Switzerland, reaching St. Gallen, but the "proper" Swiss returned him to the Germans. He arrived in Vienna with a high temperature. Following *Kristallnacht,* my concern for the family increased. Irving managed to escape to Belgium via Aachen. He did not have a visa but at least he owned a passport. He wrote to me from Brussels. I described the situation in France and he believed it would be easier to find work in Belgium. I thought that since we were both refugees it would be more sensible to stick together. It was the end of 1938. I decided to go to Belgium, again without papers, as I possessed neither a passport nor a visa. I left my belongings with one of my roommates and asked him to send them to me when I wrote from Belgium. Again my only luggage consisted of a briefcase. I traveled to Lille, crossed the Belgian border at Roubaix posing as a commuter, and made my way to Brussels.

What I did not know was that shortly before I reached Belgium the government had established a refugee camp in Merxplas. Previously a camp for vagabonds, it had been cleared for this new purpose. It lay not far from Antwerp. The Jewish Community in Brussels was urging people to go to the camp, assuring them they would be taken from there to England. Unfortunately, when I arrived in the Belgian capital Irving was already in Merxplas. I registered at the Jewish Community Center and was advised to go to Merxplas, but I chose to stay in Brussels and try my luck here. Money

Hitting Back

Working at the Belgian Merxplas camp

was even more scarce than in Chelles. I got to know the brothers K., one of whom had the nickname "Servants' Terror." They lived together in a small attic room. They let me move in with them although one of us would have to stand on the bed to open the door if we were all in the room together. The guttering went through the window of the room, so we were spared the inconvenience of always making a special trip to the toilet.

Here as well I received neither a residence permit nor work, and hardly any support. The police were stalking around the Jewish Community Center and by the end of January I landed in Merxplas. In February 1939 Irving left the camp with the first transport to the Kitchener Camp in England.[5] A few others succeeded in getting to the British Isles before the transports were stopped. Not only were we separated, but for me this was the beginning of life in the camps. It would last quite a long time.

Refugee

Compared with later camps Merxplas was bearable. There was a good deal of autonomy, we could work, and there was enough to eat. We could spend the few Belgian francs we earned from work in the camp in the canteen there. Relatives could send money and many did. Family members were allowed to visit once a month and we could also request leave from the camp. Merxplas was quite large. In addition to the living quarters and the administrative buildings there were workshops for locksmiths, electricians and carpenters. State-owned agricultural estates were also attached to the camp. The living quarters were stone structures; the floors were covered with cheap tiles that were easy to clean but cold. There were eighty beds in each barrack. The walls were covered with moralistic slogans in Flemish that were intended to lead the vagabonds back to the straight and narrow. I reported for agricultural work. Had my brother stayed I would have tried to learn to become an electrician like him.

At first I was put to work in the fields. For more than eight hours a day I was on my knees pulling weeds from the beet crops. The pay was twenty centimes an hour. Work in the stables was better paid so I applied and was accepted. I learned how to harness and look after horses and drive them on the fields. I learned how to milk cows and clean them and their stalls, how to help with the harvest, building sheaves of corn and load and unload wagons, and how to carry seventy-kilogram sacks of corn up and down narrow staircases to and from the silo. At that time I weighed about fifty-four kilos.

In the camp I met friends from Vienna, Fred (Sigi) Wallach, Dolfi Panzer, the Balban brothers and others. Merxplas was a men's camp. Most of the inmates were young, between sixteen and thirty years old; some were

Hitting Back

in their forties, but hardly any older. Youth groups were active in the camp, the largest and best organized being led and inspired by members of the Communist Youth Movement. I joined this group. We read a lot, had lengthy and intense discussions and were soon a large, well-organized community that held together within the camp. I got to know Josef Winterstein (Bauchi), Ernstl Wexberg, Kurt Herzog, Franzi Soel, Leo Trinczer and many others. These acquaintances developed into life-long friendships.

The danger of war loomed ever larger and my interest in political issues grew. The attitude of the great powers toward Nazi Germany was crucial for all of us. In September 1939 Hitler began his predatory war. Shortly afterwards some of the inmates of the camp were transferred from Merxplas to Halle, north of Brussels. We were already considered suspect foreigners and internees. For the most part our group remained together and we even gained new members: Alex Gruber, Turl Schnierer, Zalel Schwager, later also Otte-Othmar Strobl, and Moritz Fels-Margulies. I was now twenty-one years old. In Halle I was offered the position of running the canteen. This was a lucky break for the group with me, since I could take care of their needs — cigarettes, chocolate and drinks, Spa Lemonade or Spa Orangeade.

In beautiful sunshine on a Sunday in May 1940 we could see airplanes in the clear sky over Brussels. Thousands of people ran out on to the streets to watch what they thought was an aerial parade when the first bombs fell. Without any warning Germany had attacked Belgium and Holland in order to circumvent the Maginot Line — the bunkers and fortresses on the French-German border. The camp in Halle was evacuated. Carrying only our most necessary possessions (most of the men took too much) we marched in the direction of the French border. No one knew where we were going. I had distributed everything from the canteen, so at least we had enough food for the march. A few women who lived in Brussels succeeded in joining up with their husbands. Moritz Margulies' wife Ida and her baby Jeanot, who was just a few months old, joined us. We carried the baby in turns. Thousands of refugees and deportees like us joined the column.

In Enghien the stream of refugees was attacked by *Stukas* (dive-bombers) for the first time. Returning three or four times and flying low they dropped their bombs. I don't know how many were killed. The stream of people moving on was still very large. We reached Tournai where we were loaded onto cattle trains. With between sixty and eighty people in each wagon there was barely room to stand, let alone sit. Men, women, children, Jews, non-Jews, political and non-political refugees, and priests in their cowls were all jumbled up together. We had no idea what our destination was. Much of the luggage that people had hauled with them remained behind. The doors were closed and a journey into uncertainty that was to last for five days and five nights began. We had no food. We cut small holes between the wooden planks of the wagons against which we pressed our mouths to get air. For hours on end the trains stood motionless, often in the scorching heat of the sun. The night, in contrast, was bitterly cold. The necessities of nature had to be performed in the wagons. Many people lost consciousness.

It happened more than once when the train was standing that we heard screams as bayonets were thrust through the slits between the planks of the wagons. We

Hitting Back

thought it must be German soldiers. When the doors were opened for the first time after two and a half days on an open stretch of land we understood. The words *Cinquième Colonne*, fifth columnists, had been painted on the wagons. "Fifth columnists" were those who collaborated or worked for the Nazis in non-German countries before and after the invasion by Hitler. Nazi collaborators had marked the trains transporting refugees from Hitler, diverting the anger of the people from themselves to the victims of their regime.

French Concentration Camps

When the doors were opened for the first time the fresh air literally doped us. We tried to clean ourselves and the wagons as best we could. There was water. It was not easy with our stiff limbs to climb down from the wagons, and even more difficult to climb back in. On the fifth day we reached our first destination in the Haute Loire region near Vienne. The train stopped again in an open area. The doors were slid open and teams of guards stood waiting for us. Their outstretched arms were not to help us down from the wagons but rather to tear us out. We were led to a primitive camp, but compared to the transport the barracks were roomy and comfortable. There were no toilets anywhere; instead, a ditch ran through the middle of the camp. I leave the details to the reader's imagination. Nobody went too close to the ditch for fear of falling in. For reasons of modesty the priests usually slipped out there only at night, although leaving the barracks after dark was forbidden.

Everything we still possessed was taken from us on arrival and thrown together in a heap. I was already accustomed to leaving clothing behind, but what hurt me most was that my photo album was taken from me. It contained photos of my parents, my brother and sister, and friends. Despite the strict security I risked crawling at night to that building where I suspected the album to be and was lucky to find it under the pile and get back to the barracks undiscovered. I kept it under my shirt and it accompanied me through sojourns in many camps until I had the opportunity of sending it to

Hitting Back

a friend in Switzerland. After 1945 it was returned to me.

We did not stay long in this camp. The French authorities treated us as foreign enemies. Once more we were transported, again in cattle cars. This time it was less crowded and we could sit on the floor, also the doors were not completely closed so we were able to breathe. We traveled south. "South" conjures up images of lazy vacations, but this was a far cry from a holiday. The countryside from Vienne to Perpignan is indeed beautiful, but all we could see were the boarded-up sides of our wagons. Only when the train stopped did we get a glimpse of the countryside.

From Perpignan we were taken further to Elne and from there to the camp in St. Cyprien. The camp of Argelès was not far.[6] Today these towns are popular Mediterranean holiday resorts in the *département* Pyrenées Orientales. The St. Cyprien camp had been constructed for Spanish republicans who had fled Franco's terror. After the victory of Franco's Fascist regime many members of the International Brigades had been interned here. When we arrived, there was already a well-established cemetery. The camp had been built on a sandy beach bordered by the sea, a lagoon and barbed wire. The individual *îlots* were separated from each other by two rows of barbed wire between which the guards (some of them Spahis, African Lancers) patrolled. Each *îlot* had about twenty barracks that held eighty-five prisoners each. There were no beds and we had to sleep on the sand. Seven internees lay between each pair of the slanted supports of the wooden barracks (a space of about 3.5 meters). We were like sardines in a can, head to toe, but there was no other way. The days were scorchingly hot and we went about without shoes and almost

Refugee

naked, the hot sand burning the soles of our feet. At night we put on every item of clothing we still possessed. The cold sea air and the dampness of the ground penetrated everything. To add to our discomfort, the camp was infested with fleas and bugs. This situation lasted for several days until the French authorities finally comprehended that blankets, provisions, water, and the possibility for cooking had to be provided for the several thousand internees.

At first we only received cans of fatty meat and no bread or potatoes, which had the effect of a potent laxative. The wooden "toilets" could be reached by climbing a few steps. Four or five holes had been cut in the wood under which were buckets. Because of the space

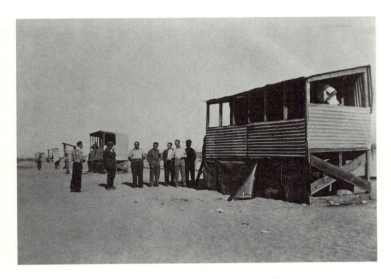

Latrines at concentration camp St. Cyprien
(courtesy of Yad Vashem, Jerusalem)

between the wood and the buckets the wind blew the urine and excrement throughout the camp. There was no paper. Old newspapers were on offer for black-market prices, like butter was towards the end of the war or immediately after 1945. I had friends in *îlot* 2. We began to adapt. Each morning the military camp administration took a roll call outside. With various tricks we usually managed to deceive the administration into believing that there were more internees than were actually present. This meant more food and later also blankets and other items.

Not surprisingly, dysentery spread through the camp. There was no medical attention, nor was there any medicine. Exposed to the infection, the camp was

Internees at concentration camp St. Cyprien
(courtesy of Yad Vashem, Jerusalem)

Refugee

defenseless. The illness began with colic stomach pains. Diarrhea and a temperature of often over forty degrees Centigrade followed. With dysentery the stool becomes watery and mixed with blood. After two or three days you are so weak that you cannot move. The disease was soon rampant and there were daily deaths from dehydration. In our barracks too, first a few, and then more and more, became ill. The healthy helped the sick to clear away the excrement; we cleaned them with damp rags and dragged them to the toilets or into the open by day if this was possible. The stench in the barracks and the whole camp was unendurable. The wind and the insects helped spread the infection rapidly. Kurt Herzog, Franzi Soel and I were among the few in our barrack who were not yet infected. We never lost our sense of humor (usually black humor) and assured each other daily that we would care for the other if he could no longer get up.

I did not get away untouched. One day at roll call I felt acute stomach cramps come over me. I tried to contain the urge to empty myself until after the roll had been taken, but as the captain on duty approached the urge was stronger than my will power. To get to the toilets could not even be considered. I lowered my trousers and crouched in the sand; after about an hour I felt a lot better. The roll call was over and no one disturbed me. I covered the traces with sand.

We got used to the daily routine of the camp fairly quickly. A camp kitchen was built. Private initiative could still flourish and "coffeehouses" with smuggled or stolen food were established in the barracks that were not fully occupied. Work teams were formed for various activities, some working outside the camp in the surrounding vineyards. It was important to work somewhere, not only for one's morale but also for the opportunity to "organize" things for oneself and for others. To "organize" means to obtain necessary items, even by illegal means, and was essential for survival. Willi Zollschan, a friend of mine from Vienna, worked in the next *îlot*. A butcher by trade he was put in the kitchens. A hole in the barbed wire (the number of holes increased with time) enabled me to slip through in my underwear. Willi provided me with strips of meat that I wound around my stomach like a belt under my underpants and crawled back to help feed our group. Even when the guards sometimes saw me they turned a blind eye to the almost naked "boy." Many French soldiers offered to share their food with us. Sometimes I was treated to pork with *garbanzos*, chickpeas; it was delicious.

Since we had neither newspapers nor radio we had to make do with the scarce information that filtered into the camp. Rumors abounded. Some people who had money or precious stones managed to escape by bribing the guards. Recruiters came from the Foreign Legion and left with new cannon fodder. One day it was announced that "Aryans" who had come from Belgium could return. Although nobody knew what or who expected him back home, most of our group were in favor of the return. It certainly had nothing to do with logic.[7] With unusual haste for the French military authorities, transport was arranged. Trains stood ready. There were enough cattle cars to hold us. They just wanted to be rid of the refugees. The "journey" was to Bordeaux via Toulouse. Bordeaux was on the demarcation line separating the German-occupied north from the unoccupied south and as such was in German hands.

What happened there in the summer of 1940 was so

Refugee

grotesque, that with the perspective of the later phases of the Holocaust it would make one laugh had it not been so bitterly serious. The German military stopped the transport at the demarcation line. The accompanying French military authorities wanted to hand over their freight — about two thousand Jews and some non-Jewish political refugees. The Germans, however, did not want them and tried to persuade their French counterparts to turn back, taking their trains and "freight" with them. The French refused "courageously and resolutely." German police and military officers checked the wagons to ascertain that they really contained refugees from the German Reich, and of course Jews. After this inspection the attitude of the Germans to the French hardened. "I am sorry, gentlemen, but we will not take Jews." We could clearly see the confusion on the faces of the Germans. The trains stood still. We could see and hear everything but had no inclination to laugh. The French went to find the SS authorities in Bordeaux, and, celebrated "victory." The SS arrived, the border formalities were quickly completed, and we found ourselves in SS barracks.

For many, the return to their original country began to appear quite different from what they had expected. Within three days the SS had separated out the political refugees and volunteer fighters from Spain. They were sent to various concentration camps (Dachau, Buchenwald, etc.). For several days a few young prisoners including myself were assigned to work on the roads. If anything irritated the SS guards they responded by lashing out with a stick or their hand. But in the summer of 1940 even the SS camp administration did not know what to do with this horde. Fortunately for us mass extermination had not yet begun.

About two weeks later all the prisoners were summoned

Hitting Back

to a roll call on the parade ground of the camp. A major of the German army mounted a provisional rostrum to address the assembled group. The SS made sure that everybody stood to attention. The slightest sign of weakness meant getting beaten. The following is a summary of the major's speech: The *Führer* had chosen an island for the Jews to which they would now be sent. The island should be cleared and made fertile. The Jews would be permitted to live there. "Aryans" and "half-Aryans" should step forward. The *Führer* had decided to allow them to return to Belgium or to their countries of origin. Apart from hand luggage nothing more could be taken. That was the speech. We had to remain standing until darkness fell and were then marched to the railway station. Again we were freighted onto cattle wagons. The whole procedure was conducted in the dark as a precaution against enemy aircraft and we could see almost nothing. It was not easy for the old or sick people to climb into the wagons. There was much pushing and shoving and the SS troops used the butts of their rifles as prods. Screams, tears and panic dominated this ghostly scene. When almost all the Jews, as well as some Catholic priests who had declared solidarity with the Jews, were tightly packed into the wagons another group of people arrived. The "Aryans" and "half-Aryans" who had been promised their freedom were also forced into the now bursting wagons. The German major and the SS had allowed themselves to play a practical joke on these people. After all, one needs to have a bit of fun every now and then, as victory after victory soon becomes quite boring!

No one knew where we were going. Some of my friends who were in the same wagon with me presumed that we would again end up in a camp in southern

Refugee

France. Most of the people in this transport were Jews from Germany. They called us defeatists when we assessed the German army and the SS as they really were. The following incident remains forever etched in my memory. While we were discussing the possibilities and the likelihood that we would probably land up in a new camp, a German Jew of about forty-five called out that we should stop talking such utter nonsense. We would be taken to an island as the *Führer* had promised. We had been told so by a German major and "a German major does not lie." Such naiveté was astonishing, considering that Hitler had been in power since 1933.

During the day the sun beat pitilessly on the wagons. With a little imagination you can picture the atmosphere inside the cattle cars. I was already an experienced rail traveler. Two German youths of twelve and fourteen sat in my corner. With a pocketknife I enlarged the gap between the planks of wood enough for us to get some air by pressing our mouths to the hole and, also, to get an idea of what was going on outside. We were correct. The destination of the journey was a camp — not a new camp — but again St. Cyprien.[8] On the wall of a barrack the following verse was written:

> *"Wir liegen hier am Mittelmeer,*
> *und haben keine Mittel mehr."*

The play on words is lost when translated, but the meaning is:

> "We lie here on the Mediterranean
> and have no means any more."

We already knew the procedure of disembarking from the train and entering the camp. This time the camp was not empty and the *îlots* and their many barracks were already occupied. We met friends and acquaintances. In addition to the strong communal spirit of our group we had considerable camp experience in "organizing." Even while the French camp authorities were carrying out a roll call, collating lists of names and allotting quarters, a few of the group who were good with their hands had disappeared to dismantle an empty barrack. They buried all the planks, stakes and squared timber in the sand. Independently and against the orders of the French authorities, who could not control the chaos, we moved into the barrack of our choice so that our relatively large and strong group could stay together. Beds were made out of the wood from the dismantled barracks so that we no longer had to sleep on the sand. The blankets that we had received in the meantime were laid out in the open each day and searched for fleas. We managed to acquire an iron cauldron from a field kitchen — illegally at night of course; legally you could only get hunger, bugs and illnesses. Every day we sterilized our eating equipment, mostly old tins from canned food, to prevent contamination.

Occasionally mail came into the camp, and in the letters some money. Most of the food provisions, especially the choicest bits, that were brought into the camp on official rations were stolen before they reached the internees. As a result we had no meat or fat. Meals consisted of a meager bread ration. The bread was massive and heavy and portioned according to weight. Sweet potatoes, usually with the soil still on them, were boiled to make soup, or if cooked with a little water distributed as a vegetable. *Karabanzen* (chickpeas) were added to the soup. If you were unlucky you would not find a single pea on your "plate." Sometimes there was fruit. I worked in a team in the vineyards and we were allowed to eat from the grapes while working. Of course we couldn't help gorging ourselves and many of us got diarrhea. But it was forbidden to bring grapes into the camp and each day we had to undergo a body check by the guards. Nonetheless we smuggled in as much as we possibly could. Being so rare, especially as very few internees were allotted outside work, it was irrelevant in what state the grapes arrived. We acquired additional food by every conceivable means. I was not quite twenty-two yet but we had among us youths in their teens who suffered from hunger far more than we did. Once we managed to obtain rice. We set about constructing a hearth using tarred paper from the roof of the barracks to make the fire. The rice was to be cooked in a flat iron pan until it was soft. We waited greedily for the extra meal. What we had not anticipated was that the tarred paper would generate an enormous amount of soot. Because of the wind, the sand and soot blew into the rice, producing a sticky, black, sandy paste. Pongo, a tall, handsome sixteen year old, was more than pleased with this concoction. Since everyone else soon lost their appetite, he consumed it all on his own. Luckily he had no negative repercussions from it.

I recognize every now and again that I am writing much more than I intended. While writing, memories flood back to me. Some I try to write down, many are lost. Most events are only meaningful when sitting with friends who were with you in the camp, with whom you shared meals and a home in the barracks. There are increasingly less of these friends and opportunities for reminiscing. Kurt Herzog, whom I met in Sydney, reminded me of numerous details and names of which I only slowly became conscious again in conversation. Possibly his life on a distant continent, isolated from his friends, contributes to his better memory.

Hitting Back

Kurt Herzog, a friend who volunteered for Auschwitz

Perhaps he is more occupied mentally with the past. Since Merxplas, Kurt has been one of my closest friends. He was never a simple character but a fellow with his heart in the right place. I do not think that he has changed much since then. He is intelligent but not practical, and tends to cynicism. I remember him then as caustic and even insulting to others, but extremely sensitive about himself. It was not egoism or narcissism but perhaps self-protection. After St. Cyprien we were together at the camp at Gurs. Our paths separated in 1942 when I left Gurs and Kurt remained until the deportations to the mass extermination camps began at the end of 1942. He could have fled but when he saw children, youths and very old people being loaded for deportation he felt it his human duty to stay with them. In effect he enrolled voluntarily as a kind of protector or organizer for the uncertain goal of this deportation, and he survived Auschwitz, Jawischowitz, and Buna. Was his sur-

Refugee

vival a reparation for his humane behavior? We met again in Vienna in 1945. Three years later he emigrated to Australia where his sister lived, his only surviving relative.

Back to St. Cyprien. Typhus broke out in the camp. In view of the prevailing conditions it spread rapidly and many died during the first days of the outbreak. Since the French guards, irrespective of rank, and the neighboring villages were also threatened by the epidemic, doctors and vaccines were brought to the camp. We were vaccinated three times, twice in the chest and once in the back. We had to line up, the needle was inserted and the vaccine injected. Nothing was sterilized and many died from an infected needle. I had a high temperature and was unconscious for twenty-four hours after the third injection. According to friends who looked after me, I was delirious and shivered with fever. I can no longer remember those hours. I got up on the second day. My fever disappeared as quickly as it had come. By the time the epidemic was over we counted several empty places in every barrack. We needed no further confirmation regarding the importance of sterilizing our eating utensils in the iron cauldron.

It was the end of August 1940 and I was with a team of workers in the vineyards when a cloudburst took us by surprise. On our way back to the camp the rain began to come down in torrents and the lanes and paths were soon covered with sludge. We waded up to our knees in water and were hit by floating wood and various household items. It was one of the few times we were actually pleased to get back to camp. The rain continued to fall heavily. What we did not know was that it was just the forerunner of a catastrophe. A terrible storm over the open sea was driving waves as tall as houses onto the shore. From the lagoon, which surrounded the left side of the camp like a half-moon, masses of whipped-up water were heading towards the camp. Guards arrived by boat and the commander rode on horseback to the camp to round up the internees to help save the camp. Sandbags had to be piled up to avoid the worst. Since he, the guards and the inhabitants of the neighboring villages faced the same danger as we did, he had no choice but to make certain promises to us.

The camp had almost become an island, with three sides surrounded by water. Gushing streams flowed down from the mountains on their way to the sea. Trees were uprooted, the foundations of houses eroded, and the houses themselves washed away. Cows, oxen and pigs were washed away with them. Many of the camp inmates were stricken with panic. The howling of the storm, the relentless rain, the landslides and the rage of the waves tore on our nerves. As our group had formed a strong sense of community we remained confident, undertaking the almost hopeless task of building a dam of sandbags against the force of nature. We had to stop working when it became dark and none of us knew whether we would live to see the next morning. We viewed the heavy rainfall as an intensification of our plight since we were now cut off from the villages. In front of us was just the roaring sea. At dawn, however, the storm that had arrived from the land side proved to be a blessing.

Thousands of tree trunks, tons of wood, dead animals including oxen still in harness, wrecked carts, mud, demolished furniture, household utensils, barn doors, and thousand upon thousand of grape vines from the vineyards were washed up on to the flat beach and had formed a natural wall, high enough to resist the waves. As daylight broke we could hardly believe we

Refugee

were safe. For the most part the camp's meager food supply had been destroyed and, as a result, instead of the promised increased rations the allocations became even smaller. Once the storm was over, we inspected the beach. We wanted to salvage from the debris anything that might be useful and haul it back to the camp. Amid the wreckage we discovered a concert piano that was badly smashed. We managed to drag it out of the wood and sludge and transport it back to the barracks. There, talented hands succeeded in recycling its mangled parts, producing a few guitars. We had often sat together singing; now we would have guitar accompaniment.

Gurs

I no longer remember the reason but it became known that the camp St. Cyprien was to be dissolved and that the prisoners were to be distributed among other internee camps. In October the time came to exchange the known harsh conditions at St. Cyprien for unknown conditions in other camps. Trucks transported us to the railway station where we were loaded onto cattle wagons. This time they were not so full and we were supplied with provisions. The train stopped several times and we were given drinking water and were allowed to relieve ourselves next to the railway tracks. The guards who accompanied the transport no longer viewed us as "fifth columnists" but as victims, like themselves, of Hitler's politics, except of course that we were *sales étrangers*. Compared to our first deportation in May 1940 this was a luxury journey. We traveled from the *département* Pyrénées Orientales along the Spanish border from the south to the southwest of France — from Perpignan past Carcassonne to Tarbes and Pau and on to Oloron St. Marie in Basses Pyrénées. We were transported by truck for the last twenty kilometers from Oloron to the camp. The new camp, 'Gurs', extended from Gurs to Navarreux, two small villages about halfway between Pau and Bayonne. The *îlots* with the barracks lay on both sides of a long road that traversed the camp. The camp was built on clay, and since rain is abundant in this district our feet sank into the mud and dirt. The camp in Gurs has been extensively described in numerous books and articles, so I will spare the reader further details.

Refugee

*Gurs: A general view of the concentration camp
(courtesy of Franz Soel)*

*Gurs: The guard and the inmates
(courtesy of Franz Soel)*

Hitting Back

Our group succeeded in staying together in Gurs as well. We were allocated *îlot* C, most of us in barrack 6. C-6 was our new address. We were not the first to be interned here and during the following months many new transports arrived. Whereas St. Cyprien had been a men's-only camp, in Gurs there were also women, but in their own *îlots*. Many German Jewish families from the area around Baden-Baden were split up and allocated different *îlots* according to sex. They vegetated in the same camp but were not allowed to be together. In St. Cyprien we had been tormented and infested by sand-fleas and midges; here bugs, lice and rats plagued us. The lice, in astronomical numbers, were the worst. People who were ill, weak or had lost their lust for life were almost consumed by them. You could sometimes find articles of clothing hanging on barbed wire or in front of the barracks in which millions of lice were intertwined. When I first saw them it made me vomit, despite my hunger and empty stomach. In our barrack we again established a "lice control." Each inmate had to present his clothing, particularly his underclothes, for daily inspection. If lice or their eggs were discovered, the piece of clothing was put into a canister and boiled. Empty tin cans or canisters served as ovens and pots for washing or cooking. If the beds were also infested with bugs sometimes the whole bed had to be burned, although it was very difficult to "organize" wood to make a new one.

The camp — including our barrack — was teeming with rats. Even our organization could not get the better of these vermin. They were deft acrobats, too crafty, and had a nose for danger. We mostly slept with blankets pulled over our heads to prevent them from running over our bodies and faces. They stole and chewed up underwear and other clothing to build their nests. We spanned string below the roof of the barracks from wall to wall and diagonally, and hung our miserable bits of clothing in the middle. The rats jumped, falling from the roof, yet still managed to get at the clothing. We had no choice but to come to terms with their presence. Abraham Hochhäuser, whom we called "Aberl," was a skilled cobbler. He impaled many rats with his leather cutter. It was a sport more than anything else and did not succeed in decimating the rat population at all. Actually I cannot help wondering whether the rats stole food from us or whether we took food away from the rats! Our meals most of the time consisted of: *citrouille* (an inferior gourd), *raves* and *navets* (beets), and *topinambours* (a type of sweet potato, but in fact a pig swill). These vegetables were stored on the clay floor of an unused *îlot* and chewed on by thousands of rats. Cooked in water, these half moldy, rotten vegetables constituted the 'soup', which for months was our midday meal.

Outside, a water pipe with a number of taps provided the only water supply for the inmates of several barracks. Winter began early that year and when the frost came the water turned to ice. Many stopped washing, did not clean their eating utensils and certainly not their clothes. Physically and morally weakened, a dozen inmates starved or froze to death each day. We would not let the winter get us down. Everything that could be burned was collected. Twice a day we unfroze the water pipe. We washed ourselves and our eating utensils before boiling the lice-infected clothing as usual. It was a cruel winter. We had only our optimism, our youth (most people in our barracks were between sixteen and thirty-five) and our spirit of community to set against the cold, the wind, the damp, the dirt and our poor nourishment. At first everything had been done to make the barrack as pleasant to live in as the conditions allowed: beds were made or repaired, and flooring was laid — even if there had to be large spaces between the planks — to avoid sinking into the clay and the dirt. Every bit of paper we could get our hands on was used to protect ourselves against the cold.

My friends and I knew that our best chance of survival lay in work. Which type of work was irrelevant. It was an opportunity to leave one's *îlot*, meet other internees, hear of comings and goings and discover whether acquaintances or relatives were among them. It was even more important to make contact with guards and people from the camp administration. The reward for the working internee was better treatment. The tangible advantages were a larger ration of bread, sometimes legume vegetables, rice or — with luck — some meat and fat. Almost everything would be brought back to the barracks and shared. One of the most important jobs was the "lavatory express." Through the disposal of excrement one could smuggle valuable things into the *îlot* and the barracks.

The first aid agency active in Gurs was the *Secours Suisse* under the leadership of Elsbeth Kasser, a big-hearted woman with tremendous courage, power and charm, who was prepared to make sacrifices and toiled endlessly on our behalf. Many of the inhabitants of Gurs owe their life principally to her and the agency for which she worked. Elsbeth lives in the vicinity of Zurich and many years later visited me a few times in Vienna. We still exchange greetings, particularly at Christmas.[9] Our contact with "Sister Elsbeth" grew increasingly stronger and closer. She visited us in our barrack and, impressed with our morale and the organizational tal-

Refugee

ent of our group, she gave some of us the opportunity of working with *Secours Suisse* for the internees — in the kitchens, the stores, the administration, distribution, etc. Above all the *Secours Suisse* brought food, medicines, blankets and clothing into the camp. The most precious items were cheese, sweetened dried milk and "Lenzbourg jam." I worked in the storage areas, more precisely in the food storage area. The office, the kitchens and the storage area stood at the upper end of the camp road. We had a permit to leave our *îlot* and enter all the others, including those in the women's camp, in the course of distribution.

Among the youngest in our barracks were Pongo, Dackel and Jean Fruhr. "Pongo" and "Dackel" were of course nicknames. Kurt Herzog, Bauchi (Josef Winterstein), Alex Gelb, the two Balban brothers from the ninth district in Vienna and Harry Herzl were about my age. Ernstl Wexberg, Ossi (Ochshorn), Turl Schnierer, Franzi Soel, Schmauchi (Glattauer), Zalel Schwager, Mäcki (Max Sternbach), Moritz (Dr. Fels Margulies), Alex Gruber, Wallach, Aberl, and Friedl Weiss were older — between twenty-eight and thirty-five years old. Karli Nassau, my school friend, lived in the same *îlot* but in a different barrack. Although he was much stronger and bigger than I, he looked terrible. I tried to persuade him to come to our barrack but he refused. I provided him with as much food as I could get hold of. The camp had robbed him, like so many others, of his moral strength and will to survive. He was transferred to the camp "Les Milles." Leon Feuchtwanger, who had been with him in the same barracks there, mentions him several times in his book *Das ungastliche Frankreich*.[10] Feuchtwanger managed to get out of this camp and get to America, Karl Nassau was deported and murdered by the Nazis.

With few exceptions there were only Viennese in our

Hitting Back

barrack. Many were Communists, Social Democrats, one was a "Krausian"[11] and of course there were plenty who had never been politically interested or active. Only the Communists were politically active. There were long discussions about the present and the future. In addition to the Swiss organization, the Jewish-French organization OSE (*Oeuvre de Secours aux Enfants*)[12] also came into the camp, as well as Abbé Glasberg,[13] Ninon Hait and, somewhat later, the young Jeannine.

Some of the male internees were selected for forced labor in the French coal mines. In one of these selection processes I was also chosen. I was tenacious, but I weighed less than forty-four kilos! My friends, such as Alex Gruber who had worked in coal mines in northern France in 1938, believed I had little chance of surviving for long. Thanks to my contacts with Ninon Hait, Abbé Glasberg intervened and succeeded in getting me released from the transport to the coal mine. Instead, I was transferred to the camp's fire service. This could hardly be described as hard labor. In practice, once allotted nobody cared what we did, or if we did anything at all. The permit and the insignia of the camp fire service provided total mobility within the camp. For a time I lived in a separate barrack near the south gate of the camp but I was still able to meet with friends in *îlot* C or those working for *Secours Suisse* and OSE. In addition I could transport things from *îlot* to *îlot* more easily than others. Naturally the fire service was on duty day and night. Patrolling during the cold nights was not pleasant and for that reason we did not take night duty too seriously. In the late hours of the morning when inspection was conducted at least four of us were in our beds as proof that we had completed the night duty.

After a few months I changed my job and became a

gardener for the OSE, and moved back to *îlot* C barrack 6. A few of us decided to supplement our poor diet by growing our own vegetables — cucumbers, tomatoes, radishes and carrots. The potential of even the most infertile soil became clear to me when the tomatoes and radishes I had planted and tended began to grow. This activity served more as occupational therapy than as a source of agricultural produce. The vegetables we managed to grow from this tiny spot of ground provided nothing more than a tidbit for a privileged few.

Our contact with Elsbeth Kasser, Ninon Hait and Abbé Glasberg, as well as with Jeannine, provided our group with a decisive advantage. In return, the good relationships that were established during their frequent visits to our barracks gave these people the necessary belief that their work had a purpose. Also, surrounded by the physical and psychological disintegration of most of the internees due to malnutrition, filth, separation from their families, despair about the present and anxiety for the future, frustration over being forced to live day and night in the closest contact with so many and such different people, I can say without presumption that we were an example to others. We worked, kept ourselves and our surroundings clean, had more or less similar outlooks and, whether justified or not, we were optimistic. That was not easy with Germany reporting one victory after the other. We wished and believed that Hitler, the Nazis and Germany would lose the war and we wanted to contribute to their defeat in some way. But we did not know what, how and when this would be.

I became friendly with Jeannine. She was a dreamer, and somehow was able in the depths of her soul to remain untouched by the misery of the camp. My

Hitting Back

friendship with Jeannine gave me a great deal: above all relaxation, shared dreams, and tenderness in a world full of violence in which I was otherwise surrounded exclusively by youths and men.

Life in Gurs had become easier for all of us. The supervision inside the camp gradually became less rigid. People were allowed to move between the *îlots*, and the segregation between the male and female *îlots* became more relaxed. It was during this time that Ernst got to know his Edith, Zalel his Mädi, and Bauchi his Rena. The three couples married after the war. They would survive the illegality, the prisons, the concentration camps in Poland, and meet each other again — in

Matchmaking in Gurs
"Bauchi" and Rena (after the War)

Refugee

Vienna. Other attachments flourished: Kurt was aflame for Senta, Ossi was passionate for Liesl, and Harry had his Pit. Sadly, none of these romances reached a happy end. Kurt survived Auschwitz and returned to Vienna after the liberation but Senta remained in France and today lives in Paris. Harry managed to flee to Switzerland but Pit was arrested in a raid and murdered by the Germans. She was very young. Liesl was deported and survived the concentration camps in Poland but Ossi was arrested by the Germans while involved in illegal activities in northern France. Later he was deported and murdered.

Agricultural "Training"

Abbé Glasberg had connections or perhaps also personal relations with the Deuxième Bureau[14] and with de Gaulle. His brother Vermont was an officer in the French army and later held high office in the *Armée Secrète* within the *Résistance*. Abbé Glasberg made every effort to get the young people out at least in the Gurs camp. With that objective in mind, he used official channels and was instrumental in creating semi-official means agreed upon by the authorities. The argument he put to the authorities was that since farmers and various businesses were short of workers due to the war, the young internees could be hired out for their labor. The groups would live together and be supervised by the local police. This workforce would remain internees and would have limited freedom of movement in their new quarters. Abbé Glasberg and Ninon Hait also had connections to "ORT," a Jewish organization concerned principally in training and retraining Jews for industrial or artisan jobs.[15] ORT was to provide tools, small machines and eventually also instructors. The third, and hidden, aspect of the scheme was to influence young people to join the Gaullist resistance movement, when called upon. At that time, the beginning of 1942, the *Résistance* was still at the stage of consolidation and more an idea than a practical reality.

The first group, to which I belonged, was formed in the spring of 1942. It was unfortunately also the last. This wonderful idea to outwit the authorities would only be realized once, at least in the camp. There were about twenty-five of us, the majority male. We were to

Refugee

Abbé Glasberg (in 1974)
(courtesy of Dr. Lucien Lazar)

work in an isolated rural area. We were allowed to take with us all that we possessed, which was not much. Abbé Glasberg accompanied the transport. As expected, a small team of guards traveled with us, holding our documents to be presented to the local police. Naturally we were envied by many in the camp and it was not easy to leave good friends behind. Jeannine wanted me to stay in Gurs for a while as she was sure she could find a way to secure my freedom and the circumstances necessary for a common future together. But I left Gurs and Jeannine behind and went with the group. Turl Schnierer was responsible for our troop. Also Austrian, he was from the second municipal district of Vienna; he was

Hitting Back

Jewish, an intellectual, a Social Democrat who became a member of the Communist Youth Movement and later belonged to the illegal Communist party of Austria. We had been together since Belgium and got along well.

We traveled by train — this time a normal passenger train with carriages and comfortable compartments — through a beautiful part of France. We journeyed from the southwest to the southeast, via Tarbes from Pau to Toulouse, then on through Carcassone, Montpellier, Nîmes, and Avignon to Aix en Provence where we changed trains for Gap. From there we were taken in trucks accompanied by police over poor mountain roads to Rosans. This small village does not even figure on most maps. Rosans and Gap are in the *département* Hautes Alpes. Rosans consisted of a few houses in the mountains at an altitude of 1200 meters, 50 kilometers from Gap. The mountains there rise to about 1600 meters. It is a dry, stony, eroded region. The rain falls on the other side of the mountain ridge into the *département* Drôme, which is very fertile. In Rosans only a few farmers still attempted to produce anything from the poor soil. Most of the houses had been abandoned and left to ruin. We were accommodated in a relatively large house in quite good repair, that had neither stables nor a barn, and we assumed that the area must have once belonged to a wealthy landowner or nobleman before erosion had made the region so infertile. A ten-minute walk up the slopes led to a wood. The next farm was almost two kilometers away.

We were not permitted to move beyond a radius of three kilometers from the accommodation we had been allocated. It was typical bureaucratic nonsense as there was no possibility of control: the police station was a

Refugee

long distance away and to reach our place of work — farming or felling trees — we had to exceed this limit. The mountain regions in unoccupied France seemed to offer some safety. Large towns or cities were more dangerous, and attempting to flee to Italy, an ally of Germany, would have been pointless. Switzerland had hermetically sealed its borders. At that time all emigrants caught by Swiss border guards were handed over to the German authorities.

We settled down in Rosans. Some worked as woodcutters, others for farmers. I worked on the farm of the Nourrissier family, a married couple with three children, the youngest a girl of four. Mme. and M. Nourrissier were over forty but appeared older, no doubt due to their many years of backbreaking farm work. Most of what was harvested went into feeding their own family. Potatoes, tomatoes, cucumbers and pumpkins were sown. There were small patches of grass, some grain, fruit trees, grape vines and a few old lime trees. I remember these particularly well because I helped pick their blossoms. We used a single pole ladder, with rungs sticking out left and right, that we placed to lean against the fork of two branches. We had sacks fixed round our hips so we could use both hands. Thousands of bees and wasps swarmed around us, but they did not seem to be bothered by our presence and we never got stung. The tools with which we worked were decidedly primitive, for example the ground was watered with watering-cans. Field work in the usual sense was not possible because of the stony ground. The farmers' most valuable assets were their sheep. M. Nourrissier often took me into the mountains to check on the sheep and see that they had enough water. He and the few other farmers who lived there had an unerring instinct as to

Hitting Back

whether and where there was water under ground. He always carried a few special water pipes with him. This simple but practical implement was a thirty-five to forty centimeter long piece of iron with one end shaped like the sharp end of a hook. He would hammer the pointed end of the pipe into the rock and after some time water would slowly begin to flow. This was collected in a trough and served people as well as animals, especially the animals. I often tried my hand at this, hammering the pipe into a crack in the rocks, but water never appeared. Yet every time M. Nourrissier — with his instinct and his practiced eye for the tiniest changes in rock formation — hammered into the rock, water flowed.

Politics and its implications were never mentioned. Mme. Nourrissier was very fond of me; it was more than maternal affection but not what you would describe as a sensual attraction between a mature woman and a youth. I felt secure and had a sense of belonging. The first time I ate snails was with the Nourrissier family, not prepared in the way I would become familiar with in good restaurants many years later, but freshly found, finely chopped and fried with eggs. One day while cleaning the mower I cut off the tip of my right index finger. The wound bled profusely and the tip of the finger hung from the nail. Apart from two children none of the Nourrissier family were at home. I wrapped a handkerchief tightly round the wound and walked the two kilometers back to our house. I remember that although I lost a lot of blood I did not panic. The wound was cleaned and bandaged. The tip of the finger grew back and today all you can notice is the scar.

Earlier than expected three men from ORT came to assess whether we met the criteria for retraining. Bauchi was quite proficient in mechanics and electricity.

Refugee

Turl named me the carpentry instructor although I had never in my life held a plane in my hands. The three men conversed with us for a long time. They believed me when I told them that I had learned my trade in my uncle's furniture factory (in reality my uncle was a construction engineer specializing in buildings and bridges, and not I but my brother had worked for him). In the meantime one of our group, S. W., sketched the cross section of a writing table, together with the profile, the vertical projection and the types of wood connections. The ORT people thought these were my drawings. We were quite taken aback when just a few days later a truck brought various tools and two joiner's benches up to our isolated mountain.

Essentially we were a politically engaged group. Political discussions were a constant ingredient of our communal life. We developed ideas and planned activities that would be pure nonsense under normal conditions. At that time though — isolated from ordinary society and living with a group of young, like-minded friends full of energy and ideas, and under the pressure of the political situation — the irrational appeared normal and natural. Turl Schnierer, who was responsible for our group, heard that metal boxes containing Marxist literature were buried under a barracks in an empty *îlot* in Gurs. These books had been hidden by volunteers of the Spanish Civil War, who had also been interned in Gurs. We decided that we needed these books and devised a plan to bring them to Rosans. A rudimentary sketch showed where the containers had been buried. Many tales describe how treasure hunters spend years of hardship and risk in the pursuit of imaginary wealth. A few books were enough to tempt us into taking an obviously unnecessary risk. I was very proud to be cho-

Hitting Back

sen for this mission. Aware of the obstacles, we considered every angle: Officially we were only allowed to move within a radius of three kilometers from our quarters, and the next railway station was some fifty kilometers away. Police controls had to be avoided, for inspections were frequent in trains and at railway stations. The region around the Gurs camp was especially dangerous. Finally, I had to find a way of entering the camp illegally (and voluntarily!), dig up the books, smuggle them out of the camp, and undertake the long journey back without being stopped and arrested.

I told M. Nourrissier that I had to report back to the camp in Gurs but had reasons for not informing the police station. I presume he did not believe me but he agreed to drive me a long distance with his horse cart. Then, for money, I managed to get a ride with a truck to the station. Again I traveled the scenic route from Avignon to Pau and from there to Navarreux. My nerves were taut and my senses alert but all went well. In Navarreux I visited a Spanish family that was expecting me. We deliberated how to get me into the camp. I knew the terrain of the camp and the routine of camp life well enough. Several exiled Spaniards lived in the vicinity of Gurs and worked in the camp; I was given a worker's overall, a Basque beret, which most of the locals wore, and a bicycle. In the early morning I rode with some Spanish workers through the south gate of the camp. The turnpike was raised, a few greetings were murmured and we rode into the camp on our bicycles. None of the guards were suspicious. It was as easy as that.

I immediately looked for my friends. I saw Elsbeth Kasser, Ninon and also Jeannine. Elsbeth, Ninon, Jeannine and a few others thought that I and Turl Schnierer, who had conceived the idea, were mad (I believe they

Refugee

were right) but were prepared to help me in any way they could. The sketchy map proved to be correct and it was not difficult to dig out the aluminum boxes and retrieve the books by Marx and Lenin. The Spaniards who had helped to get me into the camp took the books and delivered them to the family with whom I had stayed in Navarreux. But now came the difficult part. I had to leave the camp unnoticed and undertake the long journey back to Rosans with the books.

After two days in the camp with the help of Alex Gruber, Franzi Soel and a Spaniard, we hatched a plan! The northern end of the camp, where the barracks of the various aid agencies were situated, was secured with a turnpike and a small guardhouse. Guards patrolled both sides of the turnpike, on the road and in the camp. One or two additional guards were posted in the guardhouse, which had windows on all four sides. With the two packets of food that Elsbeth had given Alex Gruber, the three of us approached the camp exit. I could hear my heart pounding — not only were people most frequently inspected here, but the guard-post had a good view of the road. I was wearing the same clothes as the Spanish workers, overalls and a Basque beret. Alex Gruber walked to the turnpike with the food packets and began to speak to the guards. He wanted cigarettes in exchange for the food. That would require protracted negotiations. At the same time Franzi Soel made for the window of the guardhouse that looked out on the turnpike, so obviously that the guard in the guardhouse went to the window and engaged him in conversation. In the meantime I could creep past the unobserved left side of the guardhouse to the street side. Had I attempted to run or to walk along the road I would certainly have been noticed. I entered the guardhouse

Hitting Back

from the outside, as if I had come from the village, cleared my throat loudly and knocked on the door of the guard room. Soel remained at the window. When the guard asked what I wanted, I answered, "I'm here to visit the internee ..." (I mentioned a name). "Visits are forbidden," he replied and sent me away. Soel was still speaking to him through the window. I thanked the guard and left. Since I had come from the guardhouse the other guard paid no attention to me. A short distance further I was met by one of the Spaniards with a bicycle and I returned to the Spanish family who were keeping the books for me. With the Marxist literature wrapped in old clothing in a small suitcase I started out on the return journey. Had I been discovered in Pétain's France with this forbidden revolutionary literature, in addition to all the other factors, I would undoubtedly have been imprisoned or immediately handed over to the Germans. I arrived back safely in Rosans with these "valuable" books. One had to have enormous luck to succeed in such an escapade.

In Gurs I had been told that transports to collection camps were underway. The numbers in the camp had been decimated. A few weeks after I was back in Rosans the full-scale deportations began.

The Flight from Rosans

In August 1942 the French police under Pétain began to give massive help to Germany in carrying out its extermination program of the Jews and other opponents of the Nazi regime, irrespective of their religion. In effect the Vichy Government with their forces of "law and order" had joined ranks with their German colleagues in the still unoccupied parts of France. They were in fact accomplices in the crimes committed by the Nazis, the Gestapo, the SS, the SD and all the other German organizations.

We received an order from the police in Gap that our whole group must report to the police station with our documents, wash kit and a blanket per person. Control and registration was the reason given. We knew something was up. It was decided that only two of us, Bauchi (Josef Winterstein) and I, would go to discover what lay behind the order. At the police station we played the innocents. The commandant informed us that he had been ordered to transport us to a collection camp. After an examination we would be allowed to return to Rosans. Perhaps he even believed that. Since we had nothing with us the commandant provided a small truck and two policemen to drive us back to Rosans to collect our belongings and to return with the entire group to Gap. The two policemen were also quite ignorant. What did they know of the concentration camps in Poland and Germany or of the dangers that faced us? When the truck stopped in Rosans, Bauchi and I rushed into the house to talk to Turl. Within a few minutes a plan was devised and put into operation: Turl

Hitting Back

engaged the two policemen in a long conversation. The girls and a few of the youths in our group disappeared through the back door and hid in the nearby woods. We packed the small truck with cases, blankets and all sorts of bundles so that there was room for only a few people. The roof and sides of the truck were covered by a tarpaulin and at the back there was a low board that could be bolted. The policemen presumed that with all this equipment we were preparing for an extended stay in the camp. What they did not know was that each of us had hidden in the truck a small bag containing a towel, wash kit, underwear and some food. We purposely did not take any documents with us. Five of us climbed on to the back of the fully laden truck and the backboard was bolted behind us with some difficulty. It was clear that the two policemen would take their places on the driver's bench. Since they could not see into the back of the truck from where they were sitting we intended to jump off on the way. Each of us had memorized an address in Toulouse and in Lyon. From this moment on each had to rely on his own intuition and luck.

The five of us — Schmauchi, Jean Früh, Alex Gelb, Bauchi and myself — discussed the order in which we would jump out. I would jump first, next Bauchi and then the others at short intervals. On the mountain roads the truck drove slowly. When it reached a curve I climbed over the backboard, let myself hang down and fell. My bag was thrown after me. I scrambled quickly off the road to the slope of the mountain and lay there. Bauchi jumped soon after me. Lying next to each other we began to consider what to do.

Refugee

I would like to digress here for a moment before narrating further. While the five of us were being transported off, the others were preparing their flight. We later heard that Harry H. and Herbert K. succeeded in reaching Switzerland and survived the rest of the war there. Ernstl got to the département Drôme and from there to Lyon. Most of the others, however, were apprehended by the police at five o'clock in the morning and taken to the camp Les Milles; Turl, Mäcky (Max Sternbach), Dackel, Otto B., Pongo, Rena and Liesl were among them. As for the other three in the truck — Glattauer (Schmauchi), Jean Früh and Alex Gelb — they were caught by a search party sent out by the police, arrested and deported. Schmauchi and Jean did not survive the concentration camps. Alex Gelb has been living in Vienna since 1945.

I suggested to Bauchi that we go to the Nourrissier family for help. That was not without risk as they didn't know Bauchi and we could not anticipate their reaction, but he agreed. The Nourrissiers took us in; they did not ask much, thought practically and acted quickly to help us. We climbed a ladder to a hayloft where we were completely concealed by the hay but could still breathe. It is not difficult to imagine the events at the police station in Gap when they discovered only blankets and luggage in the truck. Needless to say it did not take long until reinforcements were sent to Rosans to fetch all of us. Hidden under the hay we could hear the Nourrissiers' house being searched and them being interrogated. We were not betrayed and the police did not find us. That night Monsieur Nourrissier suggested hiding us in a *bergerie* — a makeshift shelter for sheep. After midnight the three of us began to climb up the mountain and after an hour reached our new refuge. We crept into the darkest corner. Over the next few days the whole region was continually combed by police, sometimes with search dogs. The few farms were repeatedly searched and placed under observation. It was just as well we had not stayed in the hayloft. Mme. or M. Nourrissier found ways to bring us food and news every day. We settled in as best we could. Built roughly into the slope, the *bergerie* was a walled sheep's pen about two meters deep and four meters wide; the entrance was through an open arch about a meter and a half high and the roof wasn't much higher. Our bags served as pillows. As it was bitterly cold both day and night we stayed permanently dressed. We used the thin black coffee we were brought for shaving. During the day we stayed in our cave but at night we crept out into the open to stand up, stretch, breathe the fresh mountain air, and relieve ourselves. The food the Nourrissier family brought us included also peanuts and cooked potatoes. Bauchi was quite undiscriminating, eating the peanuts with their shells and the potatoes with their skins. Nothing could quell his innate good humor.

We had been in the sheep's pen for a week. We were squatting against the wall in our corner when the straw on the ground diagonally across from us moved. There was no wind. I poked Bauchi and whispered, "Did you see that?" "Yes," he answered laconically. We remained still. Then we saw a mouse run a few steps and heard a short whistling noise. The mouse stood on its hind legs and then fell over dead. Shortly afterwards a snake appeared and began to swallow the mouse. We knew that there were scorpions and poisonous snakes in this region but until that moment we had never been conscious of the danger. We decided to leave Rosans and informed M. Nourrissier of our decision. He brought us

Refugee

food for the journey and a sketch of how we could get to the railway station. Mme. Nourrissier insisted on fetching us a four-leafed clover to ensure our safety. With their best wishes we parted from these dear and courageous people.

Since we had no papers we had to avoid the police. We made our way only after dark. During the day we rested under the protection of trees. Despite our sketchy map we had no idea where we were going. We marched on, trusting our luck. Our shoes were not suitable for mountain walking and our feet were soon swollen and covered with blisters. On the first night after having walked for many hours we saw below us a long light streak. It had to be the road. We decided to shorten our journey and slipped rather than walked down the steep slope, but there was no road to be seen. What we thought was a road was the stripe of a field. In order not to lose our orientation altogether we scrambled on all fours back up the slope, walked a few kilometers, then collapsed exhausted on the grass of a clearing and fell asleep. When we woke up the next morning we noticed that we were less than two meters from the precipice of a steep cliff. An exaggeration, a figment of our imagination you might think. No, just phenomenal luck.

On the second night we came to a fork in the path. Bauchi studied the sketch and pronounced, "Right." After about two hours we reached a signpost that showed we were going in the wrong direction. "Let's walk back," Bauchi suggested in his characteristic laconic way. Laughing at the absurdity of it, we turned round and retraced our steps. Later that same night we were walking along a path that led through a sparse wood. The night was clear and there was enough light;

it was about two in the morning. Shortly after a bend we both stopped, rooted to the spot. About 150 meters in front of us stood two men of the *Garde Mobile*, their white leather straps across their breasts and their bags at their sides. Whispering to each other we had to make a quick decision. Should we throw ourselves to the ground, run back or walk on? Certain that they had seen us we decided to go on and trust our luck. We strode up to the policemen. Was it courage or foolhardiness? All we knew was that we were scared stiff. As we drew nearer the men of the *Garde Mobile* dissolved into nothing. What we saw was a small clearing. Light and shadow played on the branches and twigs. Nowhere were there policemen, military, or members of the *Garde Mobile*. The figures had been created by our imaginations. I have never seen a mirage but such an illusion must be similar. The fact that we both had the same vision at the same moment though was extraordinary.

We were surprised by rain on the third night of our long march. Already drenched we made for a farmyard and found a large barn whose door we could open. We entered quietly. It was August — harvest time — in the barn stood a cart loaded high with grain. We took off our wet coats and sodden shoes, crept on to the cart and lay down on the freshly cut stalks of corn. We were soon in a deep sleep. The sun was already up when we woke. We stayed where we were, following our rule never to go out during the day. Although it was Sunday the farmers were working. At about 9 A.M. some farmhands came into the barn to fetch tools. I spoke to them and explained that we had been hiking, got caught in the rain and sought shelter in the barn. Obviously this was quite plausible. They nodded and left. But we would have been stretching the plausibility if we did not move on.

Refugee

By this time it was midday and the sun stood high in the sky. On such a beautiful day young hikers would be long on their way. We could not risk that, but if we were found in the barn during the day we would no doubt be considered tramps and handed over to the police.

Just then a farmer who had seen us in the morning reentered the barn. I had to act quickly. I apologized for my lie earlier on and told him that we were from Alsace, that we had been demobilized and were to be sent to Germany to do forced labor, but did not want to work for the Nazis. We were now fleeing to relatives and could only continue our journey at night. Bauchi stood next to me and I could feel my heart pounding. Without saying a word the farmer examined us for what seemed an eternity. Then he asked: "Are you hungry?" We knew from those three words that this stranger was no source of danger. When we answered "Yes," he signaled us to stay, left and returned some fifteen minutes later with a bottle of red wine. How quintessentially French! Actually, we would have preferred bread and bacon. Perhaps he thought red wine satisfied or staved off hunger. He led us away to a nearby wood and said it would be better if the others did not find us in the barn. He described the route we should follow and where the police stations were so we could avoid them. That is all I know about this reticent farmer, yet I remain indebted to him.

We were terribly hungry. Two cans of sardines made up our last reserves. We ate them and drank the wine. We were still hungry but the wine did what wine does: we were tipsy, lay giggling in a meadow and felt pleased with life. As soon as it got dark we continued on our way. The sight of telegraph poles and wires in the distance was enough to orient us. We spent the last night of our journey in a wheat field between the upright sheaves and remained there until dawn. Our clothing was full of cut straw. We itched all over. Following railway tracks we approached a small village. It was not yet 6 A.M., the hour commuters travel to work. We wanted to reach the railway station. The main road through the village was empty, except for a tall man we spotted ahead of us. We ran up to him and, out of breath, asked where the station was. He looked us up and down and we could see in his eyes both surprise and displeasure, as if we were escaped inmates of an asylum. He raised his arm and pointed to the wooden hut in front of which we were standing. "This is the railway station," he announced, turned away and walked on.

We caught the first train to Montélimar. Abbé Glasberg had given us an address in Toulouse and another in Lyon for emergencies. In Montélimar we studied the timetable. The next train to Toulouse was not until 6 P.M., and it was now 7 in the morning. We were uneasy: in times of unrest railway stations are always particularly dangerous; they are closely watched by police and always included in raids. We saw from the timetable that in less than two hours the express from Marseille to Lyon would stop here. "Should we go to Lyon?" I asked Bauchi. He shrugged and answered, "What the hell, let's go to Lyon," as if we were about to make a day trip to St. Pölten or Vöslau, two suburbs near Vienna. We bought two tickets for first class, mounted the train, which arrived on time, and sought out our compartment. Only when we saw the well-dressed passengers did we realize the state of our appearance. We looked like vagabonds. We washed in the toilet, combed our hair, shaved and tried to straighten our clothes as much as possible. We reached Lyon without further incident.

I have already mentioned that railway stations were

dangerous. With this in mind we let ourselves be carried along with the mass of travelers to the exit and outside. Due to the gasoline shortage taxis were hard to find. I pounced on one and was about to climb in when I noticed that Bauchi was not with me. I looked round for him and saw him standing next to the horse of a hackney coach. He beckoned to me. With regret I had to leave the taxi to other passengers. Bauchi had a special relationship with horses since his childhood. His parents had owned a business in scrap metal in Hernals, the 17th district of Vienna, and they had kept horses, coaches and coachmen. He beamed at me and we climbed aboard the open *fiacre*. The address we had was of a small church in an old district of Lyon. It was a slow and never ending journey across the town. We had to cross the Rhône and the Saône, all the while listening to the coachman's lament about how weak the horses were, especially having to go so far when they were so underfed. The ride used up almost all our spare cash.

The priest of the church could not help us himself but he gave us the address of a Catholic Aid Agency back in the center of Lyon. There we should mention Abbé Glasberg. We traveled back to this new address by tram. It took us a while to find the hardly noticeable sign of the Catholic Aid Agency on the old building. We climbed up the worn steps. The staircase and the corridors were poorly lit. A man came towards us on the stairs to the second floor. He recognized us immediately. "Dolly, Bauchi," he cried, "what are you doing here?" It was Abbé Glasberg himself. He took us into his office and there was Ninon Hait. We were exhausted, but excited and relieved to be with people we knew and trusted. While he listened to our escapades Ninon made sure that we got something reasonable to eat. The

Hitting Back

first dish was jellied chicken; it was heavenly. Glasberg and Ninon gave us news of many of our friends. They also told us that police raids and arrests occurred daily and deportations were continual. Glasberg believed that we should go underground immediately. He would take care of finding a suitable hiding place. Marching a few steps ahead of us he led us to a church. There were only a few people inside. We sat in one of the front pews and waited. About ten minutes later we were fetched into the sacristy by a priest who led us out the church through a side door. He took us to the seminary of Archbishop Gerlier next to the pilgrimage church Notre Dame de Fourrière. The church, the monastery and the seminary stood on the plateau of a hill whose slopes ran down to the Saône. In addition to the old narrow path, a funicular railway ran up to the pilgrimage church. There was a breathtaking view over the whole of Lyon from the monastery and its gardens. Not far from the church grounds stood one of the oldest and largest Roman amphitheaters. Many houses in this part of the town date back to the eleventh and twelfth centuries. Our interest, however, lay not in the historical or architectural value or holiness of the place, nor in the wonderful view. What was important to us was safety, food and rest. We found just that, and the days we spent in this sanctuary were magnificent. As strange as it might sound, nuns brought us breakfast to our rooms. We ate lunch and dinner together with the seminarians. During the day we walked in the gardens. There were fruit trees and vines on the slopes and we had permission to pick the grapes and fruit.

We regularly heard news of our friends through Ninon and Glasberg and they were constantly informed about us. Not all the news was good news. We learned that many of our group had been taken to Les Milles camp. A few — Mäcky, Pongo, and Dackel — had managed to escape. Glasberg and his team of helpers succeeded in getting others out of Les Milles, among them Soel, Rena, and Edith.

We had many lengthy discussions with the seminarians on both religious and political issues. Looking back, I still appreciate today the frankness and tolerance of the student priests as we defended very contrary viewpoints during those discussions. On one subject, however, we were in complete agreement: Hitler's Germany represented a danger for all decent people. They condemned the persecution of the Jews as vehemently as they did the partial persecution of the Catholic church. I should mention that at that time many French clerics strongly opposed Hitler and the Nazis. Lyon and the South of France were not yet occupied by the Germans.

IN THE *RÉSISTANCE*

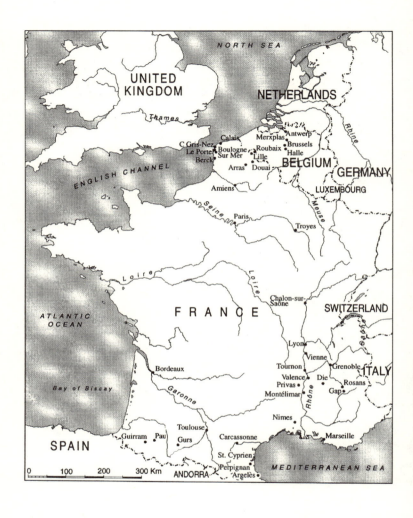

Escape from a Shelter

Glasberg assured Bauchi and me that we could remain hidden in the monastery until the end of the war. Mäcky and Dackel, for whom Glasberg had found shelter in another monastery, took up this offer and remained there until the liberation of Lyon in autumn 1944. After Mäcky's flight from Les Milles, Glasberg had arranged shelter for Mäcky with the Salesian monks. When it became known that inspections were being conducted he was forced to go underground. He rented an attic in Craponne and furnished it as a studio, where his abilities as an artist were put to use — serving not the "sublime" arts but dedicated to the production of forged documents. Aberl (Hochhäuser), a trained cobbler, built him a false floor for storing his equipment and paper. Later, for reasons of security, he rented another flat in Lyon-Villeurbanne. From his hideaway Mäcky was able to provide many active resistance workers with the necessary documents. The quality of these forgeries very often determined life or death. His achievement was invaluable.

In Paris the *Résistance* was growing and Lyon became the center of the underground movement for the *zone libre*. Supplemented by a few individuals (it is impossible to estimate the number), a group of Austrian Communists and those who sympathized with them, together with the French, built up a well-functioning organization of active resistance that had contact with key people in the *Résistance*. I knew many of them from Belgium, a few even from Vienna, and from the camps of St. Cyprien and Gurs. Neither Bauchi nor I intended to

Hitting Back

live underground until the end of the war. We were not merely concerned with our own safety; we wanted to assist actively in bringing the war to an end. We could not stand idly by while the mass murder was going on. We were intent on standing up actively against the Nazi criminals, the German murderers and their collaborators, be they in uniform or civilian clothing. We did not relish the role of the beaten and the hunted but wanted to hit back and hunt for ourselves. When we spoke of leaving the monastery to join our friends, the Abbé Glasberg protested, as did our helpers and friends in the monastery. They implored us not to put our safety at risk. At that time, September 1942, police raids and arrests were daily occurrences in Lyon.

Bauchi knew that Rena was being held in Les Milles near Marseille. We decided to give up our comfortable and peaceful life in the seminary. Since our hosts would not let us leave officially, we had no choice but to do so surreptitiously. This time we fled not from enemies but from friends, and they have long since forgiven us. We sneaked through the garden and down the slopes to the Saône, climbed over the protecting wall and were once again fair game for the police. I had received a letter from Turl Schnierer via Glasberg with the address of a Spanish family in Lyon. The family took us in and put us in touch with our friends. We asked them to contact Abbé Glasberg and Ninon Hait and to explain the reason for our abrupt and impolite departure. We were assured they understood. Glasberg was able to get Rena out of Les Milles in good time before the transports began and brought her to Lyon. She was reunited with Bauchi. He was moved to another address and I remained with the Spanish family. Two days later I received my first forged document, a *carte d'identité*. My rations card

In the Résistance

was genuine "J 3,"[1] "J" stood for *Jeunesse,* as youths were allowed more points.

I met with old friends and made new ones. We had to adapt to the changed circumstances, to acquaint ourselves with the rules of conspiracy, and to be able to slip into a different identity. In my later activity the rules of conspiracy were even stricter. The results could be disastrous if one did not comply with these rules. I remained for only a short time longer in Lyon — a period spent developing new connections. Recent arrivals had to be provided with accommodation and food, clothing and documents. One had to be particularly careful with the transport and distribution of these items. I began to prepare for my first substantial task. More effective resistance against the occupying forces was possible in the occupied zone of France. I volunteered to leave the unoccupied zone to work for the *Résistance* in occupied France. I knew that our Austrian group could take over special assignments because we spoke German. Naturally I had no idea what the exact work would be or how it would be done in practice, but neither did anyone else.

At the end of September 1942 the time came for my first assignment. Two of us were to travel together. I had met my traveling companion Billy a short time before our departure. He was from Graz and two years older than I. Paul Kessler was responsible for our travel preparations. My shoes were worn out and I also needed another suit. Egon Kodicek, a trained tailor, former Social Democrat and office holder in the trade union, took my measurements. This was done in a public toilet. The finished article was delivered to the same place. Paul also provided me with a new pair of shoes that were too tight, but there was neither time nor an opportunity to change them. Paul also gave us money and necessary information. Nothing was written down. We had to memorize everything. Somewhere between Lyon and Craponne Mäcky presented me with new papers for the *zone occupée*. At this meeting I introduced him to a new go-between, a young woman called Hélène.

We were to meet a professional smuggler at an inn in a small village near the demarcation line close to Chalôn-sur-Saône. Against payment he would take us into the occupied zone and on to the next railway station in occupied France. We found the village, the inn and the smuggler. He showed us on a map the route of the demarcation line and the way to the station. He insisted that this was necessary in case one of us got lost in the dark or if military or border guards should appear. We started out at dusk. After about two kilometers he stopped and demanded his payment. He had a pistol in his hand. We had no idea on which side of the demarcation line we were. From his directions we assumed that we still had to pass the border of the zones. He had his money and disappeared. Despite this disappointment we realized that we had got off lightly. Many smugglers worked together with the Germans; in fact at this very spot friends of mine had been delivered into the hands of the Germans. We destroyed our old papers and retained only those necessary for the *zone occupée*. Then, relying on luck, we walked in the direction we had been told. My feet were swollen and hurting as the shoes had become damp and thus even tighter. I don't know how but we found the right way and reached Paris by train. We separated in the train, each being responsible for himself, and in Paris we had different contacts.

Mine was Franz Marek.[2] We were not acquainted but would recognize each other by means of a visual sign

In the Résistance

and a code word. Our meetings took place in the rue Vercingétorix. During a walk, Franz Marek, a cool reticent character, explained what my activities would consist of. I was to become integrated in the T.A. (*Travail Allemand*). He delivered his explanations, questions and answers in a clipped military style. My orders were to travel into the "Canal Zone" in the *départements* Nord and Pas de Calais, which were known as *zone interdite* ("forbidden zone"). The German military administration had imposed particularly harsh conditions on this area. There I was to look for work in a German office in order to become active within the T.A. and to earn money to support myself. There were no further orders or details; everything else was left to my own initiative, imagination and intuition. When Franz Marek asked me whether I speak French well, I answered truthfully: "No, poorly and inadequately," to which he replied laconically, "You will learn it quickly enough." He named a street in Lille where I could meet a liaison at a fixed time each Wednesday. I impressed a further address in Lille onto my memory in case something went wrong. My liaison was a woman, at that time Franz Marek's girlfriend and later his wife, Tilly Spiegel-Marek. She maintained the connection between Paris and the *zone interdite*. I had seen Tilly only once, briefly in Gurs. My second address was that of Dr. Otto Heller. Naturally, all these people lived in Lille under false names, as I did myself. The next day, in the Jardin du Luxembourg, I was given new documents and a small amount of money. Sitting on a park bench I had time to consider what I would do. Whereas Paris had been the city of asylum for me in 1938, now, in autumn 1942, it was the city that hosted the Gestapo headquarters and the command of the German army for France.

Hitting Back

I became acquainted with my new identity. I had to forget my real name, my origins and my date of birth. From now on, I had been born in Alsace, in Andolsheim near Colmar, and my name was Jean Albert Obrecht. Hundreds of times I silently repeated my date of birth, my military service, where and when I had been demobilized, the names of my parents, the names of streets in my home town, and other details. I slipped into a different skin and had to be prepared to answer sudden questions correctly. Being from Alsace naturally I could speak German and, apart from that, I had been raised by my grandparents in Vienna. That — in a nutshell — was my biography.

At the beginning of October 1942 I began a new period of my life. Truly alone, with a new identity and under totally altered, difficult and dangerous circumstances, I traveled northwards, first to Amiens. I didn't know what I would do there but I had to start somewhere to get acquainted with my new milieu. I wandered aimlessly through the streets and tried to imagine the scenario of being stopped and questioned while eating in a café, booking a hotel room or even producing my documents. In the muddle of the millions of people in Paris the German uniforms had not been so conspicuous. Here it was quite different. It was swarming not only with regular German soldiers but also with the SA, the SS, the military police, and the French police. There were notices attached to the doors of restaurants, hotels and shops: "Entrance to Jews not permitted." Psychologically the situation was very difficult. My every nerve felt taut. I constantly had to tell myself: "That has nothing to do with you. You are not a Jew from Vienna. You are from Alsace and you are looking for work." But there was another voice, timidly asking, "Will I be

In the Résistance

believed? How will the French react when they hear my pidgin French? How will the Germans react and what will they do if my story sounds implausible? For how long will my papers stand up to examination?" Questions, fears and more questions. I would only learn the answers when put to the test.

Two days later I traveled on to Arras. There I was to make my first attempt to find a job in a German office. Unfortunately, or thank God, it was in vain — I'll never know. It still took an enormous amount of self-control to walk up to Germans, in uniform or civil clothing, and to overlook their *Heil Hitler* salute without betraying myself. From Arras I traveled to Douai, stayed just a day and went on to Lille, where I had my first meeting with Tilly. Tilly gave me money and several ration cards. She advised me to look for work in Valenciennes or Douai, and to try and find a job as a translator. The meeting lasted only thirty minutes, but showed me again that I was not alone. I had to extend the concept of belonging beyond the constraints of time and place. It no longer meant a group of people being at the same place at the same time. We were part of an underground organization. We could not and should not know about the others and had to pretend not to recognize each other at a chance meeting. Only a prearranged *treff* (meeting) was possible. In the event that we were being observed by the police or were infiltrated, these rules were crucial so that we would not betray anything in interrogation, under arrest, or expose the net of the organization if shadowed.

I traveled to Valenciennes, again found no work and returned to Douai, a small, ugly and dirty town. I spent my 24th birthday, October 15, in a tiny, unfriendly hotel room. This was no day to celebrate. I could not keep contact with any member of my family. As far as they knew, I was "missing" and remained so until the end of the war. Equally, I knew nothing of them. Wandering around the gloomy, dirty towns of the north like a gypsy was acutely depressing. I *had* to find a job.

Gradually I managed to visit German offices without, or almost without, obvious reticence and to answer questions without sweating. In Douai I realized after I had been turned down for a job that I had presented myself not to an office of the German army but to the Gestapo. Finally, two days after my 24th birthday I found work. I was employed as a laborer by a French building company that was working as a subcontractor for large German corporations on the construction of the Atlantic Wall. It was not the job I had looked for but I took it anyway.

The Germans built their Atlantic Wall in the coastal "Canal Zone" between Berck-Plage and Calais. It was a gigantic conglomerate of concrete bunkers, planned as a base for the war against Britain and as an "invincible barrier" against the threatened landing of the allied troops in France. The OKW (High Command of the German Army) together with the Organization Todt (OT) were responsible for the planning and supervision. German building companies and German engineers, architects, master builders, specialized workers, foremen, etc. were given the work of carrying out the contracts. French and Belgian subcontractors had the task of supplying thousands of "foreign workers" (from the German point of view the French in France were also foreign workers) and occasionally machines and equipment. The Germans maintained the control and supervision of the project. In practice the French and Belgian companies rented out people and equipment

In the Résistance

— a form of personnel or slave trade of the 1940s. I had to report to a work camp in Boulogne-sur-Mer and was assigned to a construction site above Enghien-Plage, some ten kilometers from Boulogne-sur-Mer.

Hitler's "Fortress Europe"

I was now a construction laborer on a deep underground digging site and lived in mass quarters for "foreign workers" provided by the Germans. The climate in the "Canal Zone" (the coast along the English Channel) is bleak in autumn and winter. My entire wardrobe consisted of a suit, some shirts, underwear and socks, as much as would fit into a large briefcase, and still the same far too tight shoes. The ground of the construction site was damp clay. During the digging operation we stood in water. After two days I could no longer wear my shoes, even after I'd removed the laces. My legs were red and swollen up to my calves. On the third day I worked in the building pit without shoes, my feet wrapped in sacking. During the day and even more so at night I froze. It was clear that I would not last much longer like this. Many people had borrowed rubber boots. I also tried to obtain some. At the end of my first week a German foreman suggested that I speak to the building director personally, which I did.

Under these circumstances I could not keep my appointment in Lille. On Saturday I went to the construction hut in which the Holzmann A.G. company and other subcontractors had their offices, and asked to speak to the building director, Mr. Kölsche. A few minutes later I was facing a large man about 1 meter 90 cm tall with wide strapping shoulders. Speaking in German I requested rubber boots so that I could work. While I spoke he studied me intently. I had grown a mustache and rather wispy sideburns to make me look older than I really was, hopefully over thirty, as my false

In the Résistance

papers stated. Being thin and weighing only fifty-two kilos, I did not have the typical stature of a laborer. To his first question, "How come you speak such good German?" I replied, "I am from Alsace." He then asked other questions concerning my place of birth and my military service, which I answered without hesitation.

Then came a surprise. He asked if I would prefer a different, less strenuous job. Restraining myself from screaming out "yes" I pretended to ponder over the suggestion. He probably misunderstood my hesitation and added that I would earn more money. I asked what this work would consist of and he elaborated — the administration of an equipment depot, which would entail distributing shovels, spades, nails, pliers but also gasoline and other items, and collecting them again. I would be working with Germans, French and Belgians and the

Building Hitler's "Fortress Europe"
(courtesy of Yad Vashem, Jerusalem)

knowledge of both languages would be useful. Apart from the fact that I could recover physically, it was of enormous advantage for my real task. I agreed, began my new job on Monday morning, and from that day was added to the wage lists of Holzmann A.G. The tools, equipment, barrels of gasoline, working clothes, shoes and boots were stored in three sheds. I took a pair of sturdy shoes and rubber boots for myself. The sheds had wooden floors and my legs recovered quickly. Theft was commonplace. Since there were shortages of everything, demand was great, and almost anything could be exchanged for food. Both the Germans and the "foreign workers" usually did not return, or only partially returned, equipment they had borrowed. Many items were reported lost or damaged. In addition, the building site was several kilometers long and not only the equipment but also the people who had borrowed it were hard to find. Military personnel, among them high ranking German army officers (even a holder of the iron cross) often came without the required vouchers and requested various items, but mainly gasoline for their private cars. I didn't really care and was generous. The stocks diminished while I was in charge but the number of my friends increased accordingly. Sometimes German officers even invited me for a meal in the officers' mess.

A new problem arose. It was November 1942 and I had no ration cards for food or clothing. I had moved out of the mass quarters, among other reasons also because I was forced to hand in some of my cards there. I found accommodation in Le Portel, a small neighboring town, and went to the town hall (*la mairie*) to register and obtain the necessary cards. The authorities asked where I had last been registered. In order to

In the Résistance

receive new cards it was mandatory to present my de-registering document issued by the town hall where I had received my previous cards. Naturally I could not bring such a document and explained that I came from the unoccupied zone and it would take some time to obtain the necessary papers by mail. In the meantime I had to eat. I was given a few cards at last until my documents with this confirmation would arrive. Three days later I moved to Wimille, a few kilometers away from Le Portel, and again went to the town hall to demand ration cards for clothes and food. I was given the same information. I returned to Le Portel and went to the mayor's office. I chatted up an official and persuaded her to write me the following letter of confirmation: "In anticipation of de-registration from the district (near Lyon) we have issued Monsieur Obrecht with food ration cards for seven days." It was dated and stamped. The official had not written anything untrue. I presented this letter, this certificate — an officially stamped document — to the mayor's office in Wimille. The young clerk there assumed that the de-registration had arrived in Le Portel. Upon presentation of my *carte d'identité*, work permit and residence registration, she had no hesitation in issuing me with a *carte de ravitaillement* and a *carte de vêtement*. At last I had something "official" in my hands.

I had missed one meeting with Tilly in Lille. A week later she did not come to the arranged rendezvous. I made use of the emergency address and found the house of Dr. Otto Heller. When the housekeeper opened the door after my repeated ringing of the bell and I asked for Monsieur X (Dr. Heller of course also lived under an assumed name) she told me hurriedly that it would be better to avoid the house. Monsieur X. had been

Hitting Back

taken away by the Germans a few days before. I was lucky that the house was not under surveillance. Dr. Heller was deported and did not survive his imprisonment.[3] The next meeting with Tilly was successful. In the meantime Turl had arrived in the *zone interdite* and would now act as my liaison. Tilly gave me the time and place I could meet Turl in Boulogne-sur-Mer.

Right from the beginning of my work administering the stores I had the opportunity to speak to many Germans as well as French and Belgian workers. This had helped me to orient myself, and to collect impressions and my first pieces of information. It was not long before Director Hermann Kölsche made me a new offer: I could work for him as a translator and establish myself in the offices of Holzmann A.G. For my real task this was an ideal solution. I became his translator, undertook all manner of office work and soon became a sort of private secretary to him. After a relatively short time I not only felt at home in the skin of Jean Obrecht, I acted and reacted more naturally, speaking and behaving as if I were someone else. Dolly Steindling was suppressed and faded. But transforming my real self was rather a long process and not without conflict. I was too often confronted with unexpected situations where it suddenly became clear to me who I really was, what role I was playing, what I had to do for my self-imposed task and what I had to hide. In effect I had to conceal four major facts: that I belonged to the *Résistance* and actively worked for them against Nazi Germany; that I had undertaken a special project within the T.A. in which Austrian Communists had leading positions; that I was Austrian; and that I was Jewish. A false move that might arouse suspicion or betray me on any one of these points would have meant falling into the German murder machinery.

In the Résistance

Jean Obrecht was the translator for the *Oberbauführer*, a chief building director, whose position was equivalent to that of a staff officer in a military headquarters and an *Obertruppenführer* in the SS. Judging by the reaction of others, particularly Germans, I recognized very quickly with what importance my job and hence I, was viewed. Already in the first days of our working together in the office the following dialogue took place:

Kölsche: "Tell me Obrecht, do you actually have an Aryan grandmother?" I was stunned by the question. After a pause I considered with lightning speed that, coming from Alsace, I did not necessarily need to know about the German race laws and answered, "What is an Aryan grandmother?" I was quite unnerved and waited, but instead of explaining to me the intricacies of this racial concept, Kölsche told me his story:

"I am from Berlin, and before 1933 I had many friends and acquaintances who were Jewish. All of them were good people of high social standing and from decent families. Many had to leave Germany. From 1936 to 1939 I lived in Brazil and worked with major industrialists for Holzmann A.G. There I met Jewish families I had known in Berlin. Of course I had contact with them, some of them were close friends. The German Embassy and the German Consulate in Rio repeatedly urged me to break off these contacts with Jews but I took no notice of them. In summer 1939 I was called back to Berlin."

With that the conversation ended. He did not seem to expect a response. He soon took me into his confidence and believed he could rely on me absolutely. Although I was enormously relieved by his attitude I still had to act my role perfectly with him.

Kölsche hated the Nazis, the SS, and the Party. For him Hitler was an upstart, a bungler who understood

Hitting Back

nothing about waging war and was therefore a danger to the Reich. Kölsche imagined a victorious Great Germany under military leadership, with the generals in power. In private he only associated with high-ranking German officers who were stationed in the Canal Zone. Almost every week he sent a crate of food, clothes, fabric and perfume home to Berlin. He told me he had a nephew who belonged to the SS, "Hitler's bodyguard." One day he showed me a letter he had written to his wife. Among other things he wrote, "... Should it ever reach my ears that you have ever given anything from all the things I send you — even a single egg — to my nephew, you should not expect any more parcels."

Looking back, I don't know why Kölsche gave me that letter to read. He did not seem to expect any opinion on it. While I write these lines I cannot help wondering if he had not hoped for more candor from me.

Bomb alerts were sounded a few times every day. British bombers were attacking positions on the coast as well as inland. At about 6 P.M. one evening while I was still at work the alarm was sounded: a few targets near Boulogne had been hit. After the all-clear I took my bicycle — I was so well off now I even had a bicycle (from the army stores of course) — and cycled to Enghien Plage. Almost the entire front of my hotel was gone, and I was staring at my room now gaping the open air. Had it been an hour later I would have been in my room relaxing after a day's work. The staircase was still intact and I collected my few belongings. I found a comfortable room to rent, with lots of light, in the attic of a house. The garden was separated from the neighbor's by a brick wall. The house belonged to an elderly French lady just under sixty who had lived in Oran,

In the Résistance

Algeria for over twenty-five years. She lived alone in the house and French friends of mine who lived in the village had recommended me to her. Both the floor and the walls of the attic room were paneled in wood, providing an ideal hiding place for illegal material and leaflets. Through my work I was able to supply many items that could otherwise only be purchased on the black market, such as meat and fat. My landlady mothered me slightly, but basically she didn't care what I did or when I came and went, and did not object to me taking people up to my room, be they girlfriends or German soldiers. She had soon understood that Monsieur Obrecht was no friend of the Germans.

Boulogne-sur-Mer and the ruins of German fortifications
(courtesy of Yad Vashem, Jerusalem)

Conflicting Identities:
Steindling and Obrecht

In the meantime, Turl, my liaison, had arrived in Boulogne. The contact functioned well. I learned from him that Ernstl Wexberg and his later-wife-to-be Edith were also in Boulogne and had infiltrated German workplaces. Through Turl I made new contacts with French friends who were active in the *Résistance*. Among them was the Joly family, with whom Turl lived unregistered. I had stayed with them once overnight, sleeping in the only free spot — the bathtub. That was a clear breach of the rules of conspiracy, as was a meeting with Ernstl Wexberg that Turl had arranged. Turl, Ernstl and I had already known each other for about four years, most of them spent in camp. The three of us never met together. It was unwise and dangerous to meet friends, but we lived constantly with danger and to be able to speak with a friend about oneself and others, even if for only half an hour, made up for a lot.

I think that the hardest part of this form of illegal activity was the masquerade and the isolation of Dolly Steindling, the real "I." Obrecht, on the other hand, was fully integrated, he had a normal job and not enough time to meet all the people, friends and acquaintances who for various reasons wanted to see him. Time was needed for the real task, and the multitude of acquaintances were ideal prerequisites for its fulfillment. Obrecht had become accustomed to associating with Germans. He felt no direct threat to himself from the various German uniforms, the armbands, the flags with the swastika, the

In the Résistance

Hitler greeting, the pictures of Hitler, the anti-Jewish slogans or the racist and jingoistic proclamations in the press.

Against this background, what did *my*—that is Dolly Steindling's — essential activity consist of? It had many facets:

1. I was to persuade Germans, above all members of the armed forces and wherever possible Austrians (from "Ostmark"), that Hitler would not win the war. I had to convince them that there was no point exerting themselves for the war and its continuation, and that they should rather contribute to shortening it or bringing it to an end. They should speak about it to people at the front and at home. I had leaflets printed in miniature on tissue paper to pass on to people whom I considered suitable. Germans who were prepared to distribute such leaflets or take them to Germany and Austria had to be found. Ten or more copies could be hidden and transported in empty fountain pens, cigarette packets, jars or tubes of skin cream, and toothpaste tubes. In order to protect the paper, the leaflets were first packed in condoms and then placed in the tubes or jars.

2. I was further involved in obtaining and passing on any information that could curtail the length of the war. These could be items of political, military, technical or organizational information. Depending on the type of knowledge, or sometimes material, I would pass this on to Turl or directly to French friends.

3. It was also an important objective to support the T.A. financially and to assist French friends by obtaining clothing, food and other commodities that the urban guerrillas needed.

Jean Obrecht had a very busy schedule too. I had to work ten hours a day from Monday to Saturday, a total of sixty hours a week, and often had to be on the building site — "le chantier" — on Sunday as well. I was in the office before 7 A.M. because in addition to my functions as translator, which took up the least amount of my time, I had a lot of office work to do. This included planning personnel work schedules for the Germans working on the building site, as well as compiling lists of the laborers who reported to work each day and their wages, calculating overtime, and reporting absence due to sickness, personal reasons or accidents. I was in charge of the documents of new employees; I would pass these on to the Organization Todt and after they had been stamped or the appropriate remark entered, return them. Various papers that had to be locked away at night were given to me for safekeeping. The head foreman Mr. Henning and I each had a key to that particular cupboard. Very important and confidential documents and drawings were kept in a safe, to which only Kölsche had access. Almost all the Germans with whom I had to deal believed that "Obrecht" was a German, and since Obrecht wore civilian clothing he was a German with special tasks. The head foreman Henning was a member of the SA. He was a difficult character and a potential danger for me, Obrecht. He was coarse, brutal and malicious. Apparently there was much about Obrecht that disturbed him, perhaps primarily because Obrecht was a confidant of Kölsche. Wherever he could, he made trouble for me. Henning's second-in-command was a member of the SS, who proudly told me more than once that he had been the first member of the SS in his home town of Speyer. But apart from that he was harmless. He was more interested in how he could earn extra money than in his duties as foreman. He knew how to cure fish and which fish were suitable, and transformed empty

In the Résistance

oil drums into ovens for smoking them. I was useful to him for my connections with both the local fishermen and the so-called foreign workers who were his most important customers. Obrecht and Speyer's first SS member got on well together. He was always prepared to show his gratitude.

All of France was now occupied by the Germans. In November 1942 the *zone libre* had also been overrun. The Germans made it clear who was in charge and that the Vichy Government no longer satisfied their security requirements. At the same time, despite their huge military power and the ever-closing Atlantic Wall, they were unable to prevent small boats from England landing night after night all along the coast of the English Channel in the *zone interdite*. These boats brought people who worked for the allies and took them back across the channel. Henning spoke to me a few times in his boorish coarse way, maintaining that because I was from Alsace I should opt for the Germans. "With the name Obrecht you are not French anyway. You should come clean." I always backed down, arguing that as a Frenchman I had served in the army and that it was my duty even after losing a war not to immediately change my nationality. Kölsche, who was present during one of these exchanges, supported my viewpoint, claiming to Henning, "A Frenchman, like Obrecht, who works for the Germans is more valuable than a German malingerer."

The bunkers of the Atlantic Wall were of various sizes, depending on their function. Concrete was usually poured once a week and a bunker had to be completed in a single casting. The casting itself often went on late into the night and the workers were paid overtime for the extra hours they put in. When the concrete was cast, technicians, engineers and high-level admin-

Hitting Back

istrators from the headquarters of the Organization Todt came to supervise the work and conduct various tests. They tested, among other things, the composition of the water and the quality of the cement (random samples). Sample castings of cement were pressure tested.

Members of the technical services of the Wehrmacht also belonged to the commission. The commission met in Director Kölsche's office where I, Obrecht, sat. Here I learned for example that sugar and aluminum cause irreparable damage, which is noticeable only after the work has been completed. I could easily pass this knowledge on and thus disrupt the German war machinery. I should mention here that I often knew when airfields were to be moved. With this information, British bombers could attack the newly assigned German runways just a few hours later.

A French girl I knew worked in the local police station. As if by chance I mentioned to her how tatty and barely legible my *carte d'identité* was. She persuaded me to get a new carte and would acquaint me with the commander. I poured ink over my documents, defacing in particular my *carte d'identité* to the extent that it was almost unusable. After it had been treated with sand, earth, the soles of my shoes and ink, it looked more like a scrap of wastepaper than an official document. I visited my friend at her place of work. The commandant asked to see the damaged *carte* and said he would issue me with a new one. I allowed myself to be persuaded. The next day Jean Obrecht possessed a brand-new *carte d'identité*, issued, stamped and registered by the police. Now I was really Jean Obrecht, an official resident of Enghien Plage. This was an inestimable improvement for my safety.

Sometimes I ate in the officers' mess in Boulogne-sur-Mer. Ernst Wexberg worked there for a short time

In the Résistance

as a waiter, but I did not know this in advance. After I saw him there I never went back. Most of the people in the officers' mess probably believed I was in the Gestapo. My civilian clothing seemed to irritate the diners and conversations turned to silence. Some time later Ernst Wexberg got a job in a military office of the German army. We met one other time in a teahouse. While we were speaking he greeted a different table and the greeting was returned. At that time I paid no attention to what appeared to be an innocuous incident.

My meetings with Turl took place several times in the house of the Joly family. I got to know them well. They were simple affectionate people who radiated supreme modesty. Without such people, the *Résistance* would have been unthinkable and would have had no chance of succeeding. At that time there were many such families and individuals. The customary concept of a hero does not fit them. Everything they did, and they did an enormous amount, was without fuss or pathos. It was as self-evident as the routine work of an office clerk. My later relationship with the Joly family was of a special kind. In their way of thinking and acting they were the epitome of numerous other honest, courageous, humane people. I, Obrecht, was fortunate to know this family.

The Joly family lived in a small house on the outskirts of Boulogne. This part of the town was sparsely populated. Through the kitchen on the ground floor you could reach the garden, which was about fifty square meters, large enough for growing lettuce and some vegetables. Behind the house was a long sloping meadow bordered at the top by a small wood. The six-member family consisted of Monsieur Lucien Joly, about fifty years old, a railway worker; Madame Terrine

Joly, also about fifty years old, a housewife, mother and grandmother; Simone, their daughter, married and about twenty-three years old, housewife and mother; Monsieur Camille, son-in-law, about twenty-five years old, dock worker; Monsieur Lucien junior, son, about sixteen years old, schoolboy; and baby Nelly, Simone and Camille's daughter. Nelly had been born premature and had been in an incubator for some time. She was not quite a year old when I first met her.

The family had a radio set, well camouflaged under a pile of coal, with which they could receive the transmissions from London. They hid pamphlets, posters, other printed material and weapons in their house. The adult members of the family served as connections,

Lucien, Terrine, and the other members of the Joly family

In the Résistance

transporting weapons and passing these as well as pamphlets on to further agents. In addition they were prepared to take in and care for people in danger. Was the Joly family not in danger? Were they not aware of this danger? They were, and they knew it. Any one of these activities could have led to the annihilation of the whole family had the German authorities become aware of any or all of them.

Thank God the Joly family survived the war unscathed. After the war we corresponded and I visited them a few times. A photograph of me stands in their living room. From my letters they discovered that my real name is Adolf Steindling but that was irrelevant to our relationship. For them I remained Jean Obrecht. Camille, his wife Simone and Nelly (already married and a mother herself) live in Boulogne to this day. I am still in contact with them, but I have lost touch with Simone's brother Lucien.

I had a short relationship with the sister of a friend (from a local family). She was about twenty, slender, pretty, and, in today's parlance, sexy. When Kölsche met her he fell in love with her and they became lovers. Naturally we saw each other often, were together again twice and afterwards remained friends without remorse on either side. This connection also increased Kölsche's trust in me.

When Director Kölsche spent a week's holiday in Berlin in January 1943 he left the keys of the safe with me. It contained building plans of the fortifications with number, size and location of the bunkers for our site. I passed the documents on to Turl one evening. By the next morning they were all back in place. For the diverse private services I carried out for Kölsche he granted me the privilege of assigning myself the same

Hitting Back

number of overtime hours that workers spent on casting of the concrete. When a bunker was cast, the working day often ended very late at night for the laborers, the German skilled workers, the foremen and the supervising personnel. Even on such days Obrecht could leave the building site at 6 P.M.

The wage lists were signed every Friday by the Director and sent to the pay office of the Organization Todt. The head foreman and SA man, Henning, knew of my privilege and naturally it was a thorn in his side. He cloaked his envy in the assertion that it would cause "damage to the German nation." On one occasion when Kölsche was ill with flu and a high temperature, Henning was replacing him. Friday came along and as usual I prepared the wage lists and calculated for myself the overtime I had not actually worked. Henning was supposed to sign it and I had to lay the wage lists in front of him. No doubt he was waiting for this moment to pounce. He skimmed over the list with no particular interest and stopped abruptly at the name Jean Obrecht. He asked in a sharp voice, "Obrecht, did you work the overtime you have listed here?" I replied softly, "No." Henning then asked, "Why do you charge it then? You have no right to do so." Obrecht answered, "Mr. Henning, I have permission to charge this overtime from Director Kölsche." Henning went red and bellowed like a bull, "Permission from Director Kölsche does not interest me. I refuse to sign! The wage list must be corrected. Director Kölsche is not here now and I am in charge. Take note of that, Obrecht!" I did not feel at all comfortable as he screamed at me but I remained fairly cool during the entire episode. I was vastly relieved when he left the office. I left everything as it was, swung myself up on my bike and rode the short distance to

In the Résistance

Kölsche's house. This was not a planned move but simply the courtesy of visiting someone who was sick. Kölsche was not alone, his girlfriend was with him. He still had a temperature. He asked what was new at the building site and I told him of the incident with Henning. That morning Kölsche had already drunk a fair amount of cognac, as medicine. When I repeated Henning's words: "The permission of Director Kölsche is of no interest to me, I am now in charge here," Kölsche was enraged. "Who does he think he is?" he screamed and downed the rest of the cognac in the bottle. He got up despite his fever, got dressed and drove with me to the office. This was clearly not about Obrecht and his overtime, but a smoldering animosity between Kölsche and Henning. I simply provided the opportunity to bring the battle to a head. Kölsche had Henning summoned and reprimanded him in front of me as if he were a new recruit. Loudly and with uncontrolled anger he addressed Henning: "Consider what you say and do. I am the director and I am in charge here. Even if I am ill I am by no means dead." Kölsche demanded the wage list from me and signed it. For him the argument was settled. It became increasingly clear to me what an untenable position I was in. As to whether the whole episode had been worthwhile, wise, sensible or necessary, the answer is a resounding "no." I could easily have avoided it by simply crossing out my overtime.

It was only a short time ago, following a conversation with a journalist who interviewed me, that I understood my behavior on that occasion. Dolly Steindling in a similar situation would not have acted that way. He would have weighed up the possible dangers. The Organization Todt employee Obrecht felt and acted completely differently.

Hitting Back

Obrecht was often not conscious that he was A. Steindling. He was aware that in performing his work for the Résistance he had to be careful, but his professional work and his perpetual contacts with Germans were a matter of course for Obrecht. For Adolf Steindling, the persecuted Jewish refugee from Vienna, it would most likely have been impossible. Obrecht and Steindling inhabited the same body, but Obrecht was an independent person, liberated from Steindling. Obrecht did not have to play a role; he was Obrecht, albeit with limitations.

Obrecht's Adventures

My meetings, contacts and conversations with German soldiers gave me a picture of what the "common man" thought about the war, the army, Hitler and the Nazis. I particularly sought out the acquaintance of "former Austrians." From conversations with them it became obvious that the majority of *Ostmärker*, as they were called by the German Reich, did not refer to themselves as Germans but as Austrians, even those who still had illusions about Germany winning the war or who supported Nazi ideology. One of my tasks was to select individuals who would be suitable for my purpose. This meant I had to be alert for signals, such as when a member of the army declared that he was fed up, cursed the war, or even expressed the opinion that Hitler would be the downfall of Germany. I had to ascertain carefully to what extent I could declare myself a French patriot and to whom I could give pamphlets to read. If individuals were willing to take printed leaflets back home with them to their own countries the handover always took place shortly before the departure of their train.

At one of the routine meetings of the testing commission for the casting of a bunker, in addition to the usual participants there was also a French contractor and his translator. The office of the French subcontractor was in the same barracks as the offices of Holzmann A.G. The translator was a young fellow, younger than I (and I was only just over twenty-four), whom I had never seen before. I watched him closely and wondered whether he had a similar task to mine. After the Frenchman had left with his translator one of the engineers working for the Organization Todt asked Director Kölsche, "Who was that young man?" Kölsche replied, "I have no idea. I only know that he is a translator for a French contractor working for us. Why do you ask?" "Oh, nothing in particular," answered the engineer, "but I noticed that he spoke German with a Viennese accent. I am from Vienna myself." They went on to talk about something else and none of those present found anything notable in this short exchange. Thankfully no one had thought of examining my pronunciation. Nothing had struck me particularly, but following this conversation I was especially attentive and when he spoke again I could clearly discern the nasal tone distinctive of the way German is spoken in Vienna. I related this incident to Turl at our next rendezvous and discovered that this was Fritz Kessler, Paul Kessler's only son. Fritz was warned and subsequently left this job. Some time later he was arrested in a police raid and deported to Poland where he survived several camps. After the liberation, shortly after the end of the war, he died on Czechoslovakian soil near the Austrian border in the most sadly ironic circumstances. With the liberation, food was good and plentiful but his body was no longer able to absorb it.

My other business required me go to Boulogne not only on Sundays and after work, but often during work hours as well. Sometimes I cycled, sometimes Germans gave me a ride in their cars. I almost always combined my journeys with official duties for the Holzmann A.G. or the Organization Todt. One day I asked a truck driver employed at the site to take me to Boulogne and back. He hesitated because he had to produce receipts for his time and journeys, and his license did not allow him to drive within the city limits of Boulogne without an extra permit. My position and its attendant privi-

In the Résistance

leges, which he enjoyed from time to time, persuaded him to drive me. At a crossing in the town area of Boulogne I signaled him to drive straight on but suddenly realized that we had to turn right — too late! A French policeman noticed this breach of the traffic rules and stopped us. The usual palaver followed: explanations of the traffic rules and explanations by the driver. The policeman pulled out his book and demanded to see our papers. A summons could have led to unpleasant repercussions for me but would have certainly resulted in the French driver losing his license, which essentially meant he would not only be without work but without the means of earning a living. I had remained silent until the policeman demanded to see our papers. The *flic* and the truck driver debated naturally enough in French. While the driver was nervously getting his papers together I leaned over him (I being Obrecht) and in the most domineering tone shouted in German: "Don't stop us; we have business to complete. Let us drive on immediately." I added a few coarse curses and signaled to the driver to put his papers away and drive on. At the first words barked in German the *flic* opened his eyes wide, put his notebook away, stood to attention, saluted and let us drive on. It had worked! We both let out a sigh of relief and laughed. The driver had no idea of course how relieved I really was. After this I did what I had set out to do in Boulogne and we drove back to the site. What might appear now as mildly amusing was actually a deadly serious event.

I did a lot of traveling in the first months of 1943. These work trips were not long but my work took me to various places between Cap Gris Nez and Berck Plage along the coast and the triangle inland, St. Omer, Lens and Montreuil. Having the necessary papers meant I

Hitting Back

could take the train. I got to Calais only later, and not by choice.

The fear of an Allied landing and the opening of a so-called second front drove the Germans to build an increasing number of bunkers for the Atlantic Wall at an increasingly hectic pace. The concrete blocks shot out of the ground like mushrooms. An incident occurred at the beginning of February that didn't involve me directly but nevertheless left me in an uncomfortable and dangerous position. A gun emplacement within the fortifications that was about to be cast collapsed. Part of the earth on which it was standing gave way, the wood tore, the iron scaffolding buckled and snapped like matches, and underground water flooded the site. There was a tremendous tumult. The news spread over the entire area like wildfire. There was talk of sabotage. Everybody with any status made a beeline for Director Kölsche. Army officers, high-ranking members of Organization Todt and people from the technical headquarters arrived with questions and proceeded to investigate the case. It did not take long until the Gestapo from Lille appeared on the scene. For hours on end everyone who worked on the site (Germans, French and Belgians) was interrogated and reports were written. Obrecht, naturally, was very busy — fetching people, translating, writing, keeping as quiet as possible so as not to arouse attention. The whole time though, I — Obrecht — was uneasy. I felt like a mouse in a trap that at any moment could snap shut on me. Later when things quieted down in the office — and I was no longer expecting it — a Gestapo man asked Kölsche, "And who is that?" He pointed at me. I could feel my nerves shaking but outwardly I remained quite composed. Kölsche answered quietly and with authority: "That is Mr. Obrecht, my

In the Résistance

translator. He works here for Holzmann A.G. I can vouch for this man myself." I believe with that he saved my life. He certainly did not know by how thin a thread my existence was hanging.

As I could never speak openly with Kölsche and after the end of the war did not seek him out (for years that would have been very difficult) I will never know what Director Kölsche, who supported a victory of the great German Empire, saw in me, or Obrecht, to explain his attitude.

One of my French acquaintances, a native Dutchman married to a French woman whose family, particularly her sister-in-law, I knew well, surprised me with "a piece of good news." He informed me that there was a girl from Alsace working in the German commandant's office in Le Portel who was — like Obrecht — from Colmar and was dying to meet me. Of course he was prepared to do anything to bring us together. I was horrified and could in no way share his enthusiasm but I had to hide my agitation. He was so engrossed in singing her praises he did not even notice my reaction. I tried to divert him, told him how little time I had and tried to postpone the meeting indefinitely. He refused to accept any of my excuses. My comment that "there must be so many people from Alsace here" met with his insistence that the girl from the commander's office knew almost no one from back home and was desperate to meet me. I let him speak and gave in. I was appalled at this "joyful" news although I had to continually reckon on this type of meeting. I knew one cannot always plan events, but I definitely did not want to meet my "compatriot." On the following Sunday I was invited by friends to lunch. My beaming hosts introduced me to Miss Siegrist, my "compatriot" from Alsace. As I had no

Hitting Back

choice I made the best of a bad job. I chatted amiably to Thérèse Siegrist, and as we were fortunately not — or at least not yet — alone, the conversation presented no problems. Her behavior suggested to me that this was not to be our only meeting. Thérèse was about twenty-five years old, my age (Obrecht was older), had brown hair, was about the same size as I but more sturdily built, not fat but stocky, rather like a farm girl. Thérèse was without doubt not the type of woman that attracted me in any sensual way. She was far too much of a "BDM-Girl," from Hitler's female youth organization.[4] She was more German than the Germans, raised as a Nazi and as a racist. She spoke of the "Fatherland," "Final Victory" and sometimes of the ruinous role of "World Jewry." I, Obrecht, began to consider this acquaintance from another angle. She worked and lived in German head-quarters: this could be extremely useful to me, that is, to the *Résistance*. But she was pro-German and that signified a certain danger for me. I had at least to neutralize her.

I visited her in her office in Le Portel where she also had a small service apartment. The offices of the commandant were open to her day and night. She invited me for a meal that she had cooked herself. It wasn't bad at all—sole fried in butter. I stayed the night. It soon became a steady relationship and I lived partly with her, without giving up my room at Enghien-Plage. Why did I maintain this relationship? There was every reason for Obrecht to develop this connection, even though he was fully aware of the strangeness of this relationship. But I, Dolly, had struggled to get work in a German company precisely because it offered such possibilities. I had achieved that, and now, in addition, I could go in and out of the German Commandant's office as I

In the Résistance

pleased. What's more, I could do so even at night. The only problem was Thérèse and her Nazi political ideas. But without her it would not have been possible. Here I was with unhindered access to important papers. I could acquire valuable permits for the resistance movement: permits to travel within the Canal Zone, permits to leave and return to the *zone interdite,* to be out after curfew, authorizations to transport heavy goods, in fact everything, and all provided with the round stamp of the Commandant's Office. The demand for such permits was enormous. With the quantity of documents I removed and passed on, the danger of my being discovered grew. But it did not come to that.

Arrest

Adolf Steindling (Dolly) did not exist. Obrecht led quite an independent life. Dangerous? Without doubt, but Obrecht by this stage had become less and less conscious of the danger. Admittedly hubris had a part in this and, as always, it had a price. Although Obrecht was only partially to be blamed, he was the one to suffer.

At the beginning of June 1943 I, that is Obrecht, had a routine meeting with Turl in Boulogne-sur-Mer. It was early in the afternoon on a warm spring day. I could see that Turl was nervous. After we had greeted each other he immediately began to explain the reason for his concern. While we walked he told me that that morning he had a rendezvous with Ernstl Wexberg near Ernstl's house but Ernstl did not show up for the meeting. Turl noticed that a truck and two cars were parked in front of the house. Various parcels had been loaded onto the truck and Germans in uniforms were going in and out of the house. Later when the cars left he went into the house and heard the sound of heavy boots in Ernstl's apartment. "I think Ernstl and Edith have been arrested," he said to me.

I, indeed all of us, had to live constantly with the possibility of being discovered and arrested, but Turl's description seemed somewhat confused and improbable. I did not want to believe it and tried to calm him. When I had run out of arguments and he persisted with his suspicion I made the following suggestion: Since I knew the German office where Ernstl worked (which according to the rules of conspiracy should not have been the case) I would go there and look. Ernstl's desk could be

In the Résistance

seen through a window on the ground floor. I thought to myself: "If Ernstl is sitting there, Turl's imagination or anxiety has run away with him. If I can't see him we'll consider what to do next." I arranged a new rendezvous with Turl and left. As I walked past Ernstl's office I looked quickly to the right and saw Wexberg sitting at his desk. I went on, much relieved, and after a few detours arrived at the place I had arranged to meet Turl. I described exactly what I had seen and said that he must be mistaken. He still believed his version of the events. We argued. After all I had known Ernstl since the beginning of 1939 and we had been in the same barracks in the same camps for many years. Turl and I arranged to meet again after I had checked on Ernstl a second time. This time the meeting place was at a barber's shop. Turl wanted to get a haircut and would wait for me. I chose a different route; walking past Ernstl's office from the other direction I glanced through the window and saw that Ernstl Wexberg was not there. But I was not overly alarmed as nobody sits at his desk all the time. I picked Turl up at the barber's and told him. He was still concerned and very nervous. He was waiting for me to make a decision. If his assumption was correct we would have to disappear at once from the coastal region and head for Paris, not even returning to our apartments. Any incriminating evidence should be immediately destroyed.

Strange as it was, I (who was I at this moment? Dolly, Obrecht? — more likely Obrecht) was not infected by Turl's anxiety, unfortunately as it was to turn out. Again we separated after setting up a third meeting and I went once more to Ernstl's office. The first attempt to look for Ernstl had been an understandable reaction from a humane and logical point of view, but it was not wise if there was the slightest suspicion that he might have

Hitting Back

been arrested. The second time was rash. The third time was irresponsible, stupid and unpardonable. Despite that I went. The wish is father to the thought: I wanted to see Ernstl and to prove Turl's suspicions unfounded and was not willing to recognize the danger. Acting like someone out for a walk, I meandered through the streets of Boulogne in the direction of Ernstl's workplace. My senses of course were on full alert and I observed every person who passed me more sharply than usual. When I passed the window my eyes wandered to the right, noting that nobody was sitting at the desk. I walked on and turned right into the next side street. What now? There wasn't even time to answer my own question. Within seconds I was surrounded by four men in civilian clothing. Germans! Secret military police as it turned out later. They spoke to me in German, demanding my papers. I answered in French. They continued in German with their tone becoming sharper. Following a short exchange among themselves they took me to a German base close by and began to interrogate and search me. The arrest was not due to chance. I had made myself conspicuous and had been observed through the very same window through which I had looked for Ernstl.

How does one behave in such a critical situation? We had heard reports of others who had been arrested. We had theoretical instructions but no training for the real thing. Was this the end? Whatever might happen I could not endanger anyone else. Could I talk my way out of it? Would sheer audacity get me out of this terrible situation? I could try, but would it work?

Thoughts were racing around in my head. Mama! I had not seen her for five difficult years. Would we ever see each other again? I had caused her worry without

In the Résistance

meaning to. But there was no time to think. They were firing questions at me that I had to answer. I had to concentrate. They had taken my coat away to search through the pockets and the lining. I was still speaking only French to gain time. But it didn't help much. My papers stated that I was from Alsace, and my identity card from the Organization Todt affirmed that I was a translator. Three people interrogated me and two searched through the contents of my jacket. They had my wallet and spread the entire contents out in front of them. They found a photo of me with a girl in the port of Boulogne; there was no doubt, from the background, where the photo was taken. Photographs in the area of the port (as well as in many parts of the prohibited area of the coast) were forbidden and punishable by death. A harmless memento for Obrecht of a short meeting with a sweet girl was evidence of espionage in the hands of the Germans.

"What is your name?"
"Where were you born?"
"Names of your parents, brothers and sisters?"
"Why did you come here?"
"What are you doing here?"
"Who are you working for?"

I repeated my memorized data automatically.

"Why did you walk past here so often? Who are you looking for? Who is with you?"

They also found leaflets in my wallet, one in French and several in German. They were appeals to German soldiers to help end the war and the Nazi regime. The leaflets were made of thin paper tightly folded. They unfolded the texts and began to read. I half sensed and half saw out of the corner of my eye what was happening diagonally behind me. In front of me were three coarse

Hitting Back

bullies, and a voice from behind me barked: "And what that is (meaning the leaflets) you don't know either?" I turned my head as if to see what he meant. His fist hit me in the face. I lay on the ground bleeding and they began to beat and kick me expertly and brutally. Teeth were knocked out. I don't remember if I felt pain; somehow that hadn't reached my consciousness. My face was smeared with blood from my nose and mouth. They picked me up, washed my face and again fired questions. I could hardly answer. They rested. An hour passed. Slowly I began to recover. They led me into the building where Ernstl had worked. It was a large room divided by a heavy curtain. In the front towards the road were two desks, one of them Wexberg's. We were in the back part of the room with a window facing a courtyard with trees. I saw a few Germans outside, some in uniform, some in civilian clothes, and Ernst Wexberg! Turl was right. Ernst had been arrested and used as bait. We were confronted with each other.

"Do you know each other?" I stared into emptiness and answered "No." Ernstl's "Yes" was more painful than the beating I had been given. We were led away. The moral slap in the face went deep and ached.[5]

Only after the end of the war in 1945, when we met in Vienna, could Ernst explain why he had answered affirmatively. One of the men standing next to him was his boss, who had greeted him and seen us together at the "irregular" rendezvous in the teahouse in Boulogne. At that time I did not know the details of this connection.

They knew my address in Enghin-Plage, I had given it to them. I knew that the apartment and my personal property would be searched for more incriminating evidence. I was taken there under the guard of the same

In the Résistance

three men from the military police, and the driver. The car stopped at the garden gate that directly faced the entrance of the house, and we entered. My landlady was more flustered than I was. One guard interrogated her and searched the lower rooms of the house. Two accompanied me into my attic room. They began to rummage through my cases, bags, the wardrobe and the drawer of my table. They found nothing. But as they started to take the bed to pieces and were about to slit open the mattress I thought about my landlady, an elderly woman. To save her unnecessary worry and the total destruction of the room, I pointed to my hiding place. I had hidden forbidden leaflets and pamphlets in the space behind the wooden wall paneling. I showed them how to take the contents out of the hiding place by lifting a plank. My candor helped (although the discovery of these leaflets incriminated me further) in as much as the Germans refrained from destroying the apartment further.

Now I would be thrown into prison. My thoughts always ran in the same direction. "I'm finished.... What will they do with me?" I was neither agitated nor apathetic, I simply saw no possibility of doing anything. The search of the house had been completed. I was taken to the waiting car.

Here I must add a short description of the house and grounds. Looking towards the house from the street, there was a strip of garden on the right and at the back of the building, and a fence separating the house from the street and the neighbors on the right. A wall about two meters high bordered the neighbor's plot to the left and back of the garden. A one-meter-wide concrete path ran around the house. The distance from the gate to the house was about a meter. When we left the house two of the guards were in front of me and one behind me. One sat himself down next to the driver, another walked round the car and sat in the back on the left. I would sit in the middle with the third guard on my right. In a fraction of a second, just as I stepped out of the front door, came the idea of running for it. Instead of taking the two steps to the car I acted instinctively, like an animal in danger, twisted away to the left, ran as fast as I could round the house, jumped up on the garden wall, trying to pull myself over to jump into the neighbor's garden and to escape from there. I had not got as far as planning how to get out of the neighbor's property. I had as good as no chance, it was a purely impulsive action but the element of surprise was to my benefit. The guards were paralyzed for a few seconds. By this time I had reached the wall, pulled myself up by my hands and supported myself with one foot to swing myself over the wall. My foot did not have enough hold, slipped and I flopped down on the wall. My advantage had been lost. One of the men had reached the wall and was already level with me. Just as I fell he shot. Two bullets hit me. My left arm started to bleed heavily and blood was running out the sleeve. They carried me into the house and lay me on the kitchen floor. My landlady's face was as white as chalk. She leaned over me and said, "You mischievous boy, what have you done?" The Germans pulled her away. Blood began to seep through my trousers; I must have been wounded at the waist, too.

I felt no pain. I lay still and observed what was going on around me as if I was a spectator and not the lead character. I was terribly tired and could feel my inner tension receding. Paradoxically I had the sensation of utter peacefulness but was still completely conscious. The guards, in contrast, were highly excited. After all,

In the Résistance

four armed, well-trained German military policemen had the order to escort an unarmed spy and deliver him alive. They were only interested in me alive; the dead can't speak. They knew as little as I as to where and how badly I had been wounded. An ambulance arrived and I was transported to a small military hospital in Boulogne, a sort of first-aid station. Although two wounds still bled I was able to move and I helped them to undress me. A doctor and two nurses approached. Slowly my mind began to work again. The doctor, or probably the nurses, would notice that I was circumcised and conclude that I was a Jew. I had fallen into the hands of the Germans, Nazis who by then had already murdered millions of people just because they were Jewish. To them I was a spy, a Communist, a resistance fighter, and, moreover, a Jew. What could I possibly hope for?

The wounds were being cleaned. The shot through the left upper arm was a flesh wound, which explained the heavy bleeding. The second wound was at the top right of the stomach. The doctor could not diagnose more than that and put emergency bandages on the shot wounds. X-rays were necessary to diagnose correctly the damage done by the bullet in the stomach, but the hospital didn't have an X-ray machine. His work was finished. My circumcision had not been noticed by any of those present. It was not much comfort but enough to give me some hope. I was taken away and transferred to the German Marine Hospital in Calais. In case the stomach wound was life threatening, I would need to be operated on immediately. The Gestapo wanted me alive. The emergency bandages were removed. I was X-rayed and thoroughly examined. Again doctors and nurses. They were more thorough, I thought, and would notice that I was Jewish; after all, the wound was right next to the circumcised organ. But again, there was no reaction and the examination was over. For the second time that day I realized that external details were overestimated at times of suppression, persecution, and a dangerous life-style.

The wounds were again cleaned and freshly bandaged, and I was taken to the ward, a comfortable, bright private room. I was not in a cast but my right leg was stiffly bandaged to the hip and I could not move it. The diagnosis was: One shot through the left upper arm. Second shot, a lodged bullet that entered the upper abdomen top right. The projectile had penetrated below the urethra and spermatic cord, entering the groin and lodged itself in the right thigh. There was no acute danger to my life. The leg had to be kept immobile. Surgery was not absolutely necessary.

The men from the secret military police had discussed the case with their superiors. I don't know why, but the group that had arrested me believed me to be a British spy, and my attempt to escape suggested that I was twice as dangerous. Responsibility was therefore transferred, and the Obrecht case was placed in the hands of the Gestapo. My room was in fact nothing more than a prison cell despite its luxury. I lay on my back — I could not have lain in any other position — and my left wrist was handcuffed to the bed. An armed guard was posted outside the room and, so that I should not feel lonely, another guard sat in my room day and night, usually with an unsecured pistol in front of him on the table. The guards rotated according to their duty roster but it was always the same marine soldiers assigned to that duty. No, there was nothing to smile about, but the bright room did affect my disposition. Things no longer seemed that grim to me. I slept well at

In the Résistance

night and it relieved both my body and soul. I remained in the hospital for five days. The handcuffs were never removed and I was not allowed to go to the toilet. The bedpan I was given brought no relief.

The guards were simple soldiers. They had been told that I was a British spy and naturally assumed that my language was English. I repeatedly attempted to get into conversation with the guard posted in my room. The simplest way was to ask them for a small favor. They never refused. They were amazed that I could speak such good, error-free German. That I came from Alsace did not fit their picture. They wanted to know why and how I came to be a prisoner here in the Marine Hospital. I told them that I had been arrested because I had been found with leaflets. When they asked out of curiosity what was in the leaflets I described the contents. To a certain extent, even though chained to my bed, I was performing my task. I remember two conversations I had with the night guards particularly clearly. Let us call my partners in the conversations "Guard 1" and "Guard 2." I must mention that none of the guards to whom I described the contents of the leaflets reacted angrily or with animosity. Neither did these two.

Guard 1 made it patently clear to me how serious my situation was. He knew with certainty that the Gestapo had a whole arsenal of possibilities to make people talk. Prisoners were not only beaten but were given drugs and chemical substances to reduce them to semi-consciousness. Under the influence of these drugs "they all break down and talk." He was not being malicious and did not want to frighten me. He was not using a form of "Nordic trickery" to extract a confession from me. The fact that the guard even spoke to me could have led to unpleasant repercussions for him. Did he want to help me? Not directly, but I should not be unprepared. He could not have imagined how this conversation terrified me. I had always been convinced that if I was ever "blown" I would never betray anyone. I began to have seeds of doubt. Can I honestly tell myself that they will not get anything out of me? I believed that I knew myself well enough to claim that the Gestapo would not manage to force me to betray anyone with conventional methods. I can endure a great deal and have steely will power. But what if the drugs neutralize this determination? Will I betray friends and place them in danger? I could not endure the moral consequences. My thoughts could not free themselves from this theme. I was extremely anxious and slept little. Only then did I realize that I was truly a prisoner of the Nazis.

I thought constantly about Mama. She was, and remains, the central figure in my life. From her I have experienced quiet, selfless love. She had given us a carefree childhood under the most difficult circumstances. She had provided us with both freedom and protection. She had character, was fair, and had a social conscience. My thoughts wandered to friends and to my brother and sister, lingered shortly with them and returned to Mama. I had to find a solution, I could not bear to hurt her. Should I pray? I couldn't pray, but in silence I begged Mama's forgiveness for what I was going to do: end my life to avoid possible betrayal. I still possessed a silver pocket watch from Vienna, from Papa. Its cover had an inner and an outer lid. My captors had omitted to take either the watch or the ring (also from Papa) that had a small ruby in the middle and tiny diamonds on each side. That night I took the watch from the cupboard by my bed, opened it and under the cover of the blankets began to bend the inner

In the Résistance

lid backwards and forwards. It was very thin and before long it broke in two. I put the watch back in its place, keeping the broken half of the lid in my hand. The rim felt like a blunt jagged knife or the blade of a small saw. I would use it to slit my left wrist. My right hand was free; the left one, which was handcuffed to the bed, was facing the wall out of the guard's sight. I turned as much as I could on to my left side and began to saw at the inside of my left wrist. It was not easy. The broken lid of the watch was not sharp enough and all it did was scratch my skin. It was difficult to keep it from slipping off my wrist and I pressed harder. The scratched skin was stinging. I had the feeling that I was sawing in the wrong place. My skin was already scratched in several places. I turned the half-moon of the watch-lid around so that I could use the point on my wrist. It bled slightly. I would have to press harder. Did I really want to do this? Yes.... No. My mind was in turmoil. In a flash-like single moment of clarity, I realized that I did want to live, I wanted to see Mama again and I wanted to tell her. I sobbed silently. I have never since had such thoughts.

With his finger on his lips, Guard 2 signaled me to whisper as I described the contents of the leaflets. After I had finished, he remained seated in the same position on his chair. He leaned slightly forward so that nobody could hear him but me. I could tell that this stranger was moved. Then he began to speak and what he said sounded almost like a confession. "I come from Berlin. My father was a member of the Communist party and was imprisoned by the Nazis in 1933. He sat for two years. Because of this my mother was not allowed to work. I also supported the Communists and often went to meetings with my father. In 1933 the Nazis let me go, perhaps because I was too young.... Hitler murders

Hitting Back

everybody, even the Germans. It is good that there are such people as you, Obrecht." And then he asked: "Do you want to escape from hospital before they come to fetch you?" He began to describe exactly the layout of the Marine Hospital, where I would be if I got out of the window and how I could escape from the hospital grounds. By speaking he was trying to clear his conscience. We could have removed the bandage from my leg, but then I asked him:

"Can you open the handcuffs for me?" (I was prepared to take the chance)

"No," came the sad reply, "The guard outside the door has the key."

"Well," I said, "I can't take the bed with me."

"When I get home leave I will tell my family about you," he said. It was a ludicrous situation. I almost had to console him. I asked him to take my watch and ring as a memento. I'd be damned if the Gestapo would get these two pieces from Papa. The next day I was fetched by the Gestapo and transferred to prison.

Prisoner of the Gestapo

My wounds were not yet healed. The bullet was stuck somewhere in my thigh and my left leg was stiff from the bandage and from lying. When the handcuffs were taken off so that I could dress myself, I got up from the bed and immediately felt a strong urge to urinate. I was escorted to the toilet and at last, for the first time in many days, could empty my full bladder. This otherwise insignificant daily event brought me more relief than can be imagined.

I was loaded onto a prison vehicle and driven to Boulogne-sur-Mer. Through the slits of the barred window I could see the streets and buildings, some of which were familiar to me, and as we arrived I mentally noted what part of town we were in. The vehicle drove into a courtyard, stopped, and the back door opened. I climbed out and was whisked away by German soldiers. I was still wearing the same clothes that I had worn on the day of my arrest—blue trousers and a gray jacket, both covered with blood stains. But the pockets were empty; they had taken everything. This time there was no office, no registration, no questions. Apparently they knew everything about me. I was immediately taken to a single cell and the door was locked behind me. I heard the heavy footsteps of the men as they left. What now? I had no idea what lay ahead of me. Above all, I did not know what the Gestapo knew about me. That they would fetch me again and interrogate me seemed certain.

Surprisingly, I felt no particular anxiety, was far from hysteria, and in the circumstances quite sanguine. Was it only two days ago that in a moment of blackness

Hitting Back

I had wanted to end my life? Yet I felt a powerful sense of hope. Why, I could not say: you can't define the undefinable. I was never a pessimist or a fatalist, but how is optimism feasible for someone who is injured, a prisoner of the Gestapo, accused of espionage and of defying military power — and on top of that a Jew? Justified or not, a positive attitude, a "Yes!" to life, generates strength. Do not give up, do not whine, if you lose your life in a just battle! Admittedly this sounds high-flown, perhaps pompous, and somewhat naive, but it shouldn't be understood as such. What I mean is that even in the most difficult circumstances where every effort seemed futile, you have to probe deep within yourself to muster that last bit of strength and forbear a little longer. The point is, *not* to give up — even in a seemingly hopeless situation.

I looked around. My "single room," my cell, was about two meters wide and four meters long. The high window in the back wall was barred but let in enough light. The furniture consisted of a folding bed, a stool with a folding table, and an iron washing table with a basin and water jug. It wasn't much but in the camps we had had even less. At about 6 P.M. the warder came, a German soldier in military police uniform. He unlocked the door, looked me up and down, and asked my name. "Jean Obrecht," I answered. "Jan," he stated, which was my name in prison from then on. The bed was unbolted and unfolded. We stepped out into the corridor where the prisoners from the other cells were already waiting with their eating utensils. I was to be taken to the toilet. The warder came with me as far as the toilet door and I was relieved to see that there was a toilet and not just a bucket. I noticed that the inmates were not wearing prison clothing. Soon after I learned that most of the

In the Résistance

occupants of this building were German soldiers convicted of criminal activities. Their uniform jackets had been taken from them and they wore drill trousers and a shirt.

My cell was on the second floor of the building. We were led to the kitchens on the first floor to get food before being returned to the cells. The courtyard could be seen from the window of the toilet and from the staircase window. Automatically I soaked up every detail, like a sponge, and stored it in my memory. Back in my cell I noticed as I took off my jacket that my wallet was still in the pocket. I couldn't fathom why they hadn't taken it; perhaps it was an oversight. Otherwise the pockets were empty and the inner lining of my jacket had been cut open. I occupied myself with the wallet, opened and closed it, touched the soft old leather, looked in all the compartments. I knew that it was empty, I was not looking for anything in particular, but the feel of this inanimate object in my hands awakened memories. Suddenly I saw something that I had not noticed in the five years of using the wallet. On the uppermost rim of a compartment in the open wallet was gold lettering. I read the name of the leather shop where the wallet had been purchased; beneath was the address, "Vienna 1, Am Graben." A piece of Vienna! But in this context not a pleasing discovery. The gold-imprinted name and address scared me and I feared that this clue had been picked up by the secret military police. I immediately tried to remove this evidence of Vienna. With that done, I had a bit more peace of mind.

The day following my admission passed: in the morning I cleaned my cell, walked accompanied to the toilet, ate breakfast; at midday and in the evening I fetched meals from the kitchen; the rest of the time I was in the cell alone. I knew in which building I was. It was a large square brick building that had been originally conceived as a mental asylum and for a long time had been used for that purpose. I knew one wing of the building from my first days in Boulogne when I had lived in mass quarters; the wing that had housed our quarters had once been the hospital of the asylum.

I realized that, as in Calais, here too the warders knew nothing about me. Since I was a prisoner of the Gestapo and therefore dangerous, I was kept in a single cell. All they knew was that they had to guard me. The next morning three men in civilian clothing were waiting for me when the cell door was opened — the Gestapo. They led me with drawn pistols to a car in the courtyard and I was taken to the Gestapo office for interrogation. I intended to say nothing and only to answer questions that were irrelevant.

There was an interrogator and a secretary. The questions began, starting with personal details:

1. Jean Obrecht
2. born 15.10.1911
3. in Andosheim
4. military service in the French army
5. from ... to ...

With several interruptions this first session lasted until about 2 P.M. I was taken back to the prison. I did not get anything to eat until evening and then it was brought to my cell. On the orders of the Gestapo I was kept isolated from the other prisoners and received "special" treatment. Every morning the cell door was opened at six o'clock and I was given a broom, a bucket, and water with which to wash myself and clean the cell. The door was locked and I was supposed to knock when finished.

In the Résistance

After this procedure I ate breakfast and was allowed to go to the toilet.

I was then fetched for interrogation. The interrogators changed but the questions almost always remained the same:

"Who are you really?"

"Where are you from?"

"Why and how long have you been in the prohibited coastal area?"

"Do you speak English?"

"Where did you get the material, the forbidden leaflets?"

"Who are your liaisons?"

"Who are your superior officers?"

"Can you read codes?"

"What technical understanding do you have about radio transmissions?"

"What did you do in the French army?"

It went on endlessly. Sometimes they shouted, other times they softened their tone. There were occasional slaps or punches from behind to the neck, the kidneys, or the back. I gave almost no answers. If I had answered all their questions, I would have had to remember exactly everything I said or surely I would have contradicted myself. From the questions I discerned that they still believed I was a British spy and it seemed they had no evidence or means to shatter my identity as Jean Obrecht. My "genuine" false papers withstood all their investigations.[6]

I have used the word "spy" several times as I was considered one by the Germans. Naturally there were spies in the war, as there are in any war. They also exist in so-called times of peace. After 1945 one speaks of agents rather than

Hitting Back

spies, although "agents" usually only spy. I distance myself from both terms and above all from what spies do. I did not act under the orders of any power, received no pay, and had no protection. There was no international law to which I could appeal. It was my personal decision. I demanded from myself that I do everything in my power to help end the Nazi mass murders and Hitler's war. There were many who thought and acted the same.

One morning, ready at 6 A.M. as always, I was not fetched for interrogation. I presumed that they were reviewing the material after two weeks of interrogation, which I hoped would give me a few days off. Although it was difficult to keep track of the days, I realized that it was Sunday. Apparently, Sunday was also the Day of the Lord for the Gestapo.

I tried to develop a closer, more personal relationship with my prison warder. He was the son of a farmer from Upper Silesia and was about my age but fairly tall and powerful. He was uncouth and not very intelligent, but in spite of his ruddy face and blond round skull he was neither brutal nor hostile. He was curious about me and asked me time and again why the Gestapo took me away for questioning every day. He was the only person who saw my condition and state of mind when I returned from the interrogation sessions.

"Jan, what do they actually want from you?" he asked yet again. I answered, "I don't know exactly myself but I was found with leaflets from the French underground movement." I took the line that the less he knew about me (from the Gestapo he had apparently heard nothing) the less significant and less dangerous I would appear to him.

"I say, Jan, how did you come by such leaflets?"

In the Résistance

"They were pressed upon me," I told him.

"You should throw such rubbish away immediately," he instructed me, to which I replied with a grimace," I know, but I didn't manage in time."

"What do they always want to know from you?"

"They always ask me the same questions, who gave me the leaflets ... but I can't tell them because I don't know the person who gave them to me."

"Yes," he said, "Don't worry Jan, they'll stop. But it may cost you three months in prison."

May God preserve his naiveté. It was better to leave him with the illusion that I must "sit" for three months than to let him know that the Gestapo would not release me alive for my "crime."

He proposed that I become his unpaid servant. He did not use the word servant, but it best expresses what my duties would be. I was more than willing to take up his offer. I knew from my camp experience how important it was to have some form of work to do irrespective of what it was. He took me to his room, which I was expected to keep clean, to wash dishes, polish his shoes, brush his uniforms, etc. I also kept in shape — alone in my cell late at night or at dawn — by doing exercises: push-ups, knee-bends, sit-ups, jumps, arm and leg movements, stretching. The gunshot wound had led to a slight stiffening of my right leg, but I had to remain mobile and keep some measure of fitness. I didn't know when I might need it.

The days passed and fortunately the nights too. The interrogations began again. The tone became sharper and the beatings increased, both in frequency and intensity, when I gave no answer. I was interrogated by the Gestapo, the military police, and military counter-espionage as well. Questions, questions, more questions. I realized that they had not yet succeeded in getting anything out of Ernstl either, which would have helped them further. I also realized that they had not caught Turl, who was in the *zone interdite*.

There was a canteen for the German guards on the first floor of the prison, just under my cell and near the kitchen. On Saturdays and Sundays the guards would go there to drink, sing, and party until late into the night. Local French women were employed there for auxiliary and kitchen work. One day, as I was being taken for interrogation, a few of these women passed by and noticed the patch of dried blood on my trousers. One of them asked me why I was locked up. I answered quickly, "Because of illegal activities. I was shot while being arrested." The guards pushed me, shouting, "Speaking is strictly forbidden." As we had spoken in French, the guards wanted to know what had been said. "They had asked if I wanted something to eat, but I refused. I get enough to eat!" I told the Gestapo. As short as this conversation was it was soon to prove immeasurably valuable.

During one interrogation I was asked for the umpteenth time the motives for my actions. But on this day the interrogation seemed to have a friendly, dignified tone. I answered, "You also had a Schlageter." (Schlageter was a German nationalist and chauvinist who carried out acts of sabotage against the French occupation force in the Ruhr region after World War I. He was executed by the French. The Nazis celebrated him as a national hero.) My response was met with silence and surprise. I was not expecting this effect, and the Gestapo people seemed impressed. For the first time I was offered a cigarette. The highest-ranking officer, who was leading the interrogation, instructed me in the fun-

In the Résistance

damental differences between Schlageter and me. In no uncertain terms they let me know that it was insolent and totally inappropriate for me to even mention the name Schlageter. Their initial surprise at my comment dissipated, but they were caught up in their own ideology and I had planted a seed in their minds.

Nothing much changed. The interrogations continued, questions were fired, and I was beaten when I didn't answer. The teams replaced each other; each had its own method but the contents remained the same. They did not suspect in the slightest that I was either Jewish or Austrian. Yet what they did know and had evidence for was enough to sentence me to death. Again and again they told me that I could save my life by giving them the names of my liaisons, the people behind me, and my superiors.

When I think of it today, almost fifty years later, I try to analyze what went on inside me during the interrogations. Somehow I succeeded in curling up like a hedgehog, apathetic, feeling the nervous tension and the beatings, filtered as if through a haze. Once back in my cell I was able to shake off this sense of numbness.

July came. My warder told me that he was going away for three weeks on home leave. "When I return, Jan, you won't be here, you'll be free. So, all the best and goodbye." I was losing not only the one person I could speak to but also the change in routine that my work as his servant had provided.

One morning I heard a sound at the door of the cell. Through the peephole I saw the face of a woman and a note was pushed under the door. I waited until I no longer heard any steps, picked up the note, unfolded it, and read it. I recognized Turl's handwriting! He and

Hitting Back

the others knew where I was, in which prison and in which cell! The first words were general and innocuous, intended to give me courage, followed by information about the Allies' landing in Sicily and Italy. "It cannot last long until Europe is liberated. Stick it out! The woman will come again, you can give her messages — René." "René" was Turl's code-name. There was no doubt that the smuggled letter came from him. What an intoxicating feeling to know that even behind these walls I was not alone; I had not disappeared; I had friends who sought and found a way to reach me despite the risks. "The note must disappear," flashed through my mind. I folded it tightly and stuck it like a fish bone into the collar of my shirt. Later I would flush it down the toilet. My brain began to work again. Was it a trap? Had they arrested Turl? Who was the mysterious woman? Was the Gestapo trying to soften me up? I managed to calm down only after breakfast and after having flushed the note down the toilet. Lacking pencil and paper, I couldn't write a message to the outside, and from a deep sense of caution wouldn't try to obtain any. It might have been a trap and I couldn't risk betraying myself. I dared not leave the cover of my tortoise shell. But underneath I was in high spirits. Without question, the short note had a profound effect on me and I felt strengthened and hopeful.

Days later there was again a noise at the cell door, the same woman's face in the peephole. She was prepared to take a written message out. We looked at each other. I made a V-sign with my fingers: Victory! I never saw her again. This simple courageous woman was one of the auxiliary workers who had asked me why I was in prison. She had passed on my answer and a description of me. This reached the Jolys and Turl and they, in turn,

In the Résistance

sent me news through her. Only those who knew what those terrible times were like can know how much this woman had risked, and I hadn't even known her.

My life as a prisoner continued. I remember one interrogation particularly well. As always they insisted that I name names. My silence really angered the Gestapo people. On that day I was beaten more viciously than usual. I fell from the chair, was kicked, pulled up, and hit again. My nose and mouth bled. My neck and kidneys received most of the blows. What was I to do? I racked my brains. I wished I would faint, but I didn't lose consciousness. "Who are your superiors?"

Always the same question. Not from clarity of thought but because by this time I no longer cared, I uttered two names: General de Gaulle and General Giraud. Would my inquisitors consider themselves mocked? Would they notice the disdain? Would they beat me all the harder? I was astonished by their response: they asked me to repeat the names. Naturally I did not know their addresses. A statement was written which I — Jean Obrecht — signed.

Now, while I write, I ask myself how one could endure this, but at the same time I know that others suffered even worse treatment, and in comparison mine was quite mild.

At the end of July 1943 the soldier from Upper Silesia, my warder, returned from leave. "Well, well, Jan, still here?" he asked. I shrugged and nodded my head. "Starting tomorrow you will clean my room again, and thoroughly, man." I was happy that he spoke to me and that I had somebody to speak to. In the late afternoon of the following day he fetched me (his valet) and led me to his room. Perhaps he noticed that I stopped and stared out of the window at the staircase a few seconds

Hitting Back

too long. Did he see something in my expression? Suddenly he called out, "Man, don't do anything stupid, don't try to escape. I always carry a loaded pistol on me and I'm a good shot!" He removed the safety catch from his weapon and trained it on me. "No, no, don't worry," I assured him, "I had enough the first time. I hope to go free soon." He laughed and put his gun away and I cleaned the dirt from his room.

The Flight

I continued doing my exercises in the cell, especially sit-ups and stretching. I asked myself what the point was. I tried to suppress all thoughts of escape, but I couldn't help wondering whether my friends outside would find a way; could they devise a plan and carry out a raid to free me? It didn't seem likely. I was beset by illusions, daydreams and hallucinations. Yet deep within, I nursed a vague hope and an intense desire to survive.

It was a Saturday in the middle of August (I could no longer remember the exact date), a day no different from others. It was evening and I was lying on my plank bed trying to sleep. This was impossible because of the noise coming from the canteen one floor beneath me — loud music and singing. The Germans. The warders drank, laughed, and shouted all night. It sounded as if they were having a good time. This reveling went on until dawn, and then finally faded into absolute quiet. I sensed the silence almost physically. I had no idea what time it was. I lay staring at the ceiling. Dawn broke and automatically (my inner clock still functioned) I got up, washed, and dressed. I sat waiting on my bed. Soon there would be breakfast. It occurred to me that it was Sunday: no Gestapo. Far off I heard the scraping steps of the warder. Suddenly and without any prior thought, I took off my jacket and shoes, slipped under the blanket and pretended to be asleep. It was neither reason nor knowledge that led me to take certain actions, but pure instinct that probably derives from subconscious motives. The cell door was opened. I lay in the same position. My warder was surprised, "Well, well, Jan, still in bed?" His

Hitting Back

voice betrayed the drunken carousing of the previous night. Rubbing my eyes I answered, "You made such a din last night I couldn't sleep." I grabbed my food bowl and put it in his hands as if this was familiar practice.

The usual Sunday morning routine was as follows: my cell door was opened; cleaning equipment was placed on the cell floor; the cell door was closed. The other cells were then unlocked and the doors remained open. My "colleagues" in the block could clean their cells, speak to each other in the corridor, and smoke. Accompanied by two or three wardens, a few prisoners distributed breakfast to the rest of the inmates. They returned to their cells and the doors were locked. When no one was left in the corridor I was escorted to the toilet and given a coffee-like drink that I took back to the cell. The door was closed and locked behind me. But this Sunday was different. My warder already had a few bowls in his hands and he took mine too. He left my cell door open behind him. I was now wide awake. My brain and my instincts were in full gear. I listened as his steps receded and faded. I jumped out of bed, put on my jacket and shoes, and walked in the direction of the toilet. I had to pass the staircase. It was quiet and all I could hear was the drumming of my heartbeat. I sneaked down the stairs to the first floor. So far nobody had noticed me. I continued down to the ground floor. I saw the gate to the inner courtyard. As if in a trance I moved on. There was always an armed sentry in front of the gate. I had walked through this gate often enough with Gestapo men on either side of me on the way to interrogation. I saw the guard — not the stiff and alert watchdog I was familiar with, but a schnapps-ridden corpse sprawled on the steps asleep. I perceived it all but wondered if I was dreaming. Past the sentry, across the

In the Résistance

courtyard to a slope beyond, and down the slope I moved. In front of me was the wall. I had often looked down on it from above and tried to estimate its height; my brain had registered approximately two meters. But standing directly in front of the wall I saw that it was higher, possibly three meters. There was no way I could scale it. I stared at it, frozen with disappointment and terror. I had literally come up against a brick wall.

A Yiddish adage came to mind: "If God so desires, even a broom can shoot." In this case the broom was a ladder! I noticed a small wooden tool shed. Next to it, leaning against the wall, there was a ladder. The unlikelihood of such a scenario would be smiled at in a farce. But I didn't feel like laughing. Spotting the ladder, climbing it and jumping down onto the other side of the wall was one thing. Having landed on the other side I tried to get my bearings. I still couldn't hear anyone in pursuit. I was now in another yard and about fifteen meters ahead of me was the outer wall. This was even higher than the wall of the inner courtyard and shards of glass were embedded in the concrete at the top. I looked around like a hunted deer and saw a sentry box whose roof was almost as high as the ledge of the wall. All my senses were aimed in one direction — away from here. I had no idea whether there was a guard in or in front of the sentry box. Thinking was pointless and time-consuming, I had to act. With no other option, I ran quietly to the back of the sentry box, clambered onto the roof and climbed onto the wall, cutting myself on the jagged glass. My hands hurt and began to bleed. One glance told me the street was empty. I jumped, fell, got up, and ran. It was about six o'clock Sunday morning and the town was asleep. After a few hundred meters I stopped running. My brain signaled: "Running draws attention; it is wiser to walk quickly." My legs followed these orders. I had to cross the town to get to the Joly's house. The shortest route led through the city center, past buildings that were occupied and guarded by Germans. Would it work? Dear God, let me succeed! Walking quickly — running — walking, the rhythm of my pace constantly changed and my breath was short. I already saw the slight incline of the lane leading up to the Joly's house. I stopped and looked around. Nobody was following me. I continued walking, looking behind me but discovered nothing suspicious. I had to think about the Joly's safety as well. As much as I wanted to, I did not steer directly to the house.

I rushed past the house to the meadow behind, which sloped slightly and offered a good view of the lower-lying houses and lanes. There was nobody to be seen and no sound. Now I could risk it. I stood at the front door and rang the bell. Madame Joly opened it. She cried out with surprise and joy "Jean?" She immediately closed the door behind me. My knees, indeed my whole body, gave way and I sank to the floor in the small hall. I was not unconscious but I was unable to speak. The family gathered around me and tried to help me up.

I was still on the floor but my sense of humor seemed to have returned. My first words were, "You said I should visit you one Sunday — well, here I am." The tension evaporated. They urged me to go up to the bedroom and lie down, but my legs refused to carry me. I couldn't get up the stairs. Monsieur Joly led me into the kitchen and I sat down. I marveled at how one's nerves function: had the Jolys lived two kilometers further away or more, I was certain I would have made it (that is, if there was no one after me). As long as I was on the run I did not feel the exhaustion. Yet the moment I reached safety my

In the Résistance

strength deserted me. Slowly I recovered. I was given something to eat and I answered their questions. Madame Joly and Simone hugged and kissed me — a lost son had returned home. A few hours later I was able to climb the stairs; the muscles of my legs were as hard as granite. A soft bed! I fell on it exhausted and slept.

I learned that "René" (Turl) was no longer in Boulogne.[7] It was not by chance that the kitchen worker could give news of me — the Joly family and René had asked dozens of friends in the *Résistance* to look for me. Without hesitation and not for a moment did the Jolys consider their own problems or the additional danger in which they placed themselves by looking after, protecting, and saving me. My escape had long been noticed and there was a warrant out for my arrest. They searched for me through the newspapers and with public posters. The Joly family was firmly and unitedly determined to protect me. I was given the room in which Turl-René had slept. According to Terrine and Lucien senior (Mme. and M. Joly) I was to stay with them until the end of the war. A real mother could not have been more kind, loving, or self-sacrificing than Terrine Joly.

How many people had already contributed, and would in the future contribute, to my staying alive? Was my situation not proof that nihilism and stereotyping have no justification?

The dead cannot speak. Perhaps that is another reason I feel it my duty to narrate my biography.

The German occupation forces had in the meantime proclaimed that the missing "Jean Obrecht" had been found and executed. This lie was their way of demonstrating to the local people that it was impossible to

Hitting Back

escape from them. I listened to Radio London. Lucien and Camille told me the daily news. The contacts and connections of the various departments of the *Résistance* were operating smoothly. The organizations in Paris and Lyon had already heard of my successful escape. I experienced peace and security and felt genuine happiness when I played with little Nelly during the day, held her in my arms, and sang to her. I was soon an integrated member of the family, enjoying their special brand of care and protection. The war was far from over. In fact it had become even more intense and more horrific. The mass extermination of Jews was being perfected, and thousands upon thousands were dying in concentration camps and on the battlefields fighting the German Fascists. I could not stand on the sidelines. The task I had set for myself was not yet over. I could say to myself: "Enough, you have done your duty. Have a rest," but this thought did not even arise, rather, I discussed with Lucien Joly what had to be done to get to Paris. Terrine and Simone in particular did not want to hear of it. "Stay here. Stay with us. Be sensible. You know they are looking for you," both women pled constantly. It would have been logical to hide out at the Jolys. I deeply appreciated their concern and their limitless hospitality, but sense and logic had nothing to do with this.

I stayed for almost three weeks. The prison, the Gestapo, the beatings and the wounds were all behind me. I already had a rendezvous arranged in Paris. My departure had been decided upon. Lucien cut my hair very short, almost military style, and my mustache and sideburns were shaved off. The next morning I was to appear at a villa about fifteen minutes walk away. Everything else was to be arranged from there.

Back to Activity

Parting was difficult for all of us: for me because I had the good fortune of knowing such people and having them as friends and because of Nelly, whom I had grown to love like a little sister; for the Joly family, especially Terrine, because they didn't want me to put myself in danger again. I studied the route and stamped the house in my mind. I wanted to go alone the next morning, but Lucien insisted on accompanying me.

The clothing in which I was arrested and in which I escaped was at the Joly's. They gave me clothes: thin trousers, a sweater and an overall to wear on top of it, and a Basque beret. I had no documents. Lucien was also dressed in overalls with a Basque beret. We were two laborers on our way to work. At five o'clock in the gray of the morning we left, Lucien a few meters ahead of me as a sort of advance column to secure the way. I suppressed my nervousness and anxiety. Lucien stopped for a moment, signaled to a house (a villa with a garden), made the V-sign, and walked calmly on. Throughout the journey we had not spoken a word. I walked towards the house and opened the garden gate. Through the darkened window on the ground floor I saw a dull glimmer of light. Most probably I was being observed from inside. I barely finished knocking when the door opened. I said that I had come from Lucien and Camille; that was enough. I was led into a large salon where two young Frenchmen of about twenty-five were waiting. We spoke softly. I had no idea who they were. They did not seem to belong to the house, but I had the impression that this was not the first time they had been there. We were given a substantial breakfast. The villa appeared to be very large and was tastefully furnished. The owners belonged to the aristocracy I presumed. I had never been in such a house before; the people I knew in Vienna who were well-off, or even wealthy to me, lived in large apartments with four to six rooms, but not in villas. As my eyes took in the sumptuous furnishings, an attractive woman of about fifty, the owner of the house, came in and greeted us. I was given a suit, new papers, money, a new name, and a 6.5 caliber pistol together with a short explanation of how to use it. I had never before held a weapon. A shopping bag was prepared. At the very bottom lay small firearms, then potatoes, two chickens, and, at the top, vegetables that partially hung over the rim. Two of us left — two young men bringing home food from the countryside into town. Our destination was Lille.

The episode in the Villa had impressed me deeply. Everything was well organized and went calmly according to plan. Each person knew what he had to do. The owners of the house must have been influential people who held key positions among the Gaullists in the area. We reached Lille, sat in a bistro, and waited for our liaison. I was in shock when I saw two of the men who had arrested me. They hadn't noticed me and walked inattentively by. Danger was always so near. A man sat down with us and a few words were exchanged. He gave me a ticket for Paris, accompanied me to the station, and waited until the train set in motion. It traveled far too slowly. The usual checks were conducted — ticket check, French police, Germans — but I did not attract attention. Finally I arrived in Paris. I walked past the barrier behind a huddle of German soldiers. Paris! I was familiar with the streets, but the weapon in my pocket

In the Résistance

disturbed me. My rendezvous was to be daily at 5 P.M. at the Bonne Nouvelle metro station. The meeting was successful. There was not much time for conversation and I described briefly, but precisely, how I succeeded in escaping. I was again given an address where I could stay for a few days and was told that I would receive new personal documents. Obrecht no longer existed. I was transformed into "Siegrist"; that was Thérèse's surname. I was certain that this name was not uncommon in Alsace.

My readiness to undertake a new assignment was ignored. I realized that my flight had aroused suspicion in the organization. Had I perhaps been freed deliberately as a decoy? Was I knowingly or unknowingly leading the Gestapo to the organization? Certainly there had been such cases, but in my case it was utterly untrue.

The organization in Lyon was to decide whether, and how, I was to be re-integrated. I left my pistol in Paris. Decked out with new papers Monsieur Siegrist traveled to Lyon. The first thing I planned to do there would be to meet my old friend Bauchi. A certain junction, where Rue X and Rue Y cross, was our meeting place. My journey to, and the arrival in, Lyon went according to plan. The rendezvous, however, was less successful. I made my way to Rue X and walked along it in search of the intersection with Rue Y. I walked up and down the entire street several times, but couldn't find Rue Y. I was sure I had correctly remembered the street names. Survival was dependent on such trivial details. I searched for and found a publicly displayed street map with an alphabetic index and grid, located both streets on the map, and discovered that rather than crossing they ran parallel to each other. Where and how would I find Bauchi? I remembered that a year before, in 1942,

Hitting Back

before I had left Lyon for the north, the Rue Paul Bert and the adjoining side streets had been a favorite meeting point. I walked to Rue Paul Bert and wandered along it. My eyes were everywhere. I carefully studied all the people I passed, but did so inconspicuously. Suddenly I flinched. Something had struck me but I didn't know what it was. I looked round and saw a young man but was certain I didn't know him. What was it about this man that was so familiar? And then it struck me. It was the jacket he was wearing. It was a sign to me to follow him. There was no doubt about it, it was the jacket Turl wore in Boulogne. Directly or indirectly this man must have gotten the jacket from Turl. In that case he must have something to do with the Organization of Austrians. I addressed him and we immediately recognized each other. It was Fritz (Albert) H., liaison for the contact to Paul Kessler. And with that I was re-integrated into the Lyon group.

I was well accepted, trusted, and many in the organization were friends from earlier times. I got to know many more in the next few months as I took on a leading role in the Lyon group. It was the time when many comrades were prepared to become illegal agitators and take on organizational activities against the Nazi regime directly in Austria — in the "Ostmark" — and in Vienna. With false papers they registered as Frenchmen at German recruitment centers that were hiring foreign workers for various jobs within the Reich. They traveled in closed transports to Vienna, Linz, or Graz. Some of them — men and women — were already in Vienna and I desperately wanted to continue my work there. From today's perspective it was pure madness — but what was not madness in September 1943 with the war at its fiercest and the "Final Solution" of the Jewish question underway?

In the Résistance

Fortunately for me, at that time the leader of the Lyon organization was "Lucien" (Oskar Grossmann). He had fought on the side of the Republicans in Spain against Franco and had practical war experience. He knew that I had been injured and that a bullet was still lodged in my thigh. Lucien explained to me that it would be absolutely senseless to send me to Vienna because the foreign body in my leg could lead to unforeseen complications. The consultation of a doctor or a stay in hospital would signify certain death. A few months later it became clear that he had helped to save my life with his caring yet thoroughly objective attitude. He himself became a victim of the Gestapo. I will come back to that later.

I lived in a rented room. The work in Lyon was quite different from my activities in the *zone interdite*. Here various organizations carried out sabotage—armed attacks on German institutions, on factories, and on transportation. At the same time, we conducted information campaigns at German lodgings, wrote graffiti on barrack walls, and distributed leaflets and posters. Forged documents, ration cards for food and clothing had to be arranged and passed on, and accommodation found for underground activists. Police raids were a daily event. Entire districts of the town were sealed off. People in restaurants and cinemas were searched. The Vichy police worked together with the Germans, and the hunting down of Jews intensified. In many police raids "suspicious" men were ordered to lower their trousers to see whether they were circumcised. Arrests, deportations, and executions were now commonplace in Lyon. My landlady believed I was an employee. I left for work daily at 7 A.M. and returned home about 6 P.M.—a "usual" working day. A different routine might have provoked questions that would have been difficult to answer. Every day, irrespective of the weather, I was faced with the problem of how to fill the time without drawing attention to myself.

It was the 15th of October 1943. Was I really only twenty-five years old? These were not happy days; there was nothing to celebrate. A short time later I caught a cold, which developed into the flu, with attendant sore throat, headache, and high temperature. I could not stay in bed in my rented room, since my landlady would call a doctor and would want to notify my employers. I had no choice but to wander around — sweating, freezing, and feverish — counting the minutes until it became dark so that I could return to my room and crawl into bed. Twice, with difficulty, I escaped a police raid, once thanks to the courageous and quick-witted Walter Ardel. Walter, about the same age as I, worked on a German air force base near Lyon. While walking together we were stopped; our papers were demanded. Walter swayed and collapsed onto the sidewalk. I realized this was a ruse as his papers were in order. As both policemen stooped, I ran and disappeared.

My shot wound announced its existence and I felt a sharp pain in my right leg. I limped home, but with each step I felt pain in my hips as well. I tried to ignore it and to hide it from others. This became increasingly more difficult, since it impaired my freedom of movement; even lying in bed at night did not provide relief. Staying in a rented room in the town was obviously a risk. Paul Kessler found me new quarters in a small village some fifteen kilometers outside of Lyon. Martha J. lived there; she knew a few people and had found a family who agreed to take me in. This family, a couple and their two daughters, owned a charming house. The father, a colo-

In the Résistance

nel in the French army, was a laureate of the *Légion d'Honneur* and a supporter of de Gaulle. A Jewish emigrant family from Prague was already living there under false names. The colonel knew that I belonged to the *Résistance*. My friends in Lyon tried to find a doctor who would examine me and operate if necessary. In the meantime I enjoyed things I had missed for a long time — good food, safety, the security of a family, the peace of the countryside, having people to talk to, and not being alone — not to mention the two daughters, Pierrette and Françoise. Living under the same roof, these young women easily set my thoughts racing to other pleasures. There were enough opportunities to be alone with either of them. My liaison with Pierrette lasted, with unavoidable interruptions, for over a year, until I eventually left France for good.

A suitable doctor was found who was willing to examine me and to keep silent about certain details. This surgeon opposed Hitler, French collaborators, and the persecution of Jews. He was told that I was a Jew who had been shot while trying to escape from a transport to a concentration camp. He examined me in his private clinic and determined that a minor operation was necessary to remove the bullet. Since the hospital personnel could not be informed, the operation would have to be performed on an out-patient basis. He gave me an appointment for 11 A.M. on a Thursday (it was at the beginning of December 1943) in the hospital Hôtel de Dieu, which was on the bank of the Rhône in the center of Lyon. Of his own free choice, and against the rules of conspiracy, Walter Ardel accompanied me to the hospital. Moreover, he promised to keep an eye on the hospital gate until he was sure that I was capable of getting to the railway station alone. According to the doctor, the operation would take less than an hour. But as it happened, things turned out differently.

The Surgery

The surgeon was punctual. My leg was X-rayed but no print was made, so as to avoid leaving evidence. Marks were drawn on my thigh. We went to the outpatients room: a table, instruments, the doctor and a nurse. I undressed and was given an injection of local anesthetic. After a few preparatory sterilization procedures the surgeon began to cut. I was wide awake and watched. The incision was at the front of the right thigh near the groin. The doctor assessed that the bullet lay not very deep. The nurse worked very nimbly — dabbing, cleaning, and passing instruments. The first clamps were in place. The scalpel dug further into my flesh. The pain was excruciating. I sweated profusely and gripped the table tightly so that I wouldn't scream. But I was unable to prevent my muscles from cramping and my leg from jerking. The nurse gave me another two injections and the pain receded. The surgeon worked on. He dug a little deeper, and deeper still, with the scalpel. The clamps held the wound open. I didn't know how much blood I had lost; it seemed a huge amount. I could feel every muscle in my body. Every nerve, not only those where he cut, transmitted the pain to my brain. The doctor watched me. Loss of consciousness, or a partial, even transitory, failure of an organ would have created difficulties for him. I was immobile, in pain and semi-conscious, but determined to use all my willpower to save him from any such danger. He signaled to the nurse for another injection but no more had been prepared. She went off to fetch and sterilize a syringe. It was almost

Hitting Back

noon. The doctor was not sure in which direction to cut further.

What had been intended was no longer feasible. He had to make new arrangements that surely put him and me at risk. He instructed the nurse to take me to the X-ray room and prepare the room for surgery. The board of the X-ray machine was lowered to a horizontal position and served as the operating table. Time and again he led the disk of the machine to my thigh, examined the exact position of the bullet, and with intense concentration continued to cut. With both hands I grasped the sides of the table. Every now and then I had to loosen my grip as the brass fittings conducted electricity, or had I been hallucinating? I was certainly conscious and could see exactly what was going on.

There were no more injections. In their place I got encouraging words from the surgeon. Perhaps he needed them as much as I did. Did any of this concern me? The pain reminded me that it did. Otherwise it was as if I were experiencing the operation third hand. In addition to the nurse there was also an orderly, but it was the surgeon's skill and experience that would determine the outcome. He observed me when he lifted his head for a moment and I noticed his solemn and worried face. I wasn't sure for whom I felt sorrier — the doctor or myself. The pain was unbearable; it was driving me to the verge of insanity. Until put to the test, you cannot imagine the limit of your endurance. Only my muted and suppressed groaning signaled to the doctor that I was still conscious.

The surgeon straightened his back; this and the look of relief on his face indicated that he had been successful. He touched me gently and said that he had located the bullet and it was now simply a matter of

In the Résistance

extracting it. The nurse handed him a forceps. The wound was large and deep. The numerous attempts to insert the forceps to grip and pull out the bullet flooded me with waves of excruciating sensations for which the word "pain" is too mild. But the bullet was immersed in a bath of pus and could not be extracted. The doctor laid his instruments aside, pulled off his rubber glove, shoved his hand into the wound, grasped the lump of metal, pulled it out, and let the *corpus delicti* immediately disappear. Only then could my muscles begin to relax. My entire body twitched convulsively. I had made it!

Because of the abscess the wound couldn't be closed. A bandage was placed over it, then a towel, and finally a sheet folded to a width of about forty centimeters was wrapped around the leg. The doctor informed me that I couldn't yet walk; in this state he couldn't allow me to leave. I would have to stay in the hospital. The leg had to remain immobile for about ten days and the pus allowed to clear. "Give the nurse your documents, ration cards, etc. She would take care of the formalities for you," he said, adding, "I have already had a bed prepared for you." It was half past one. The operation took two and a half hours. During this time the doctor had battled, had not given up, and had not left me in the lurch. In addition to the immense concentration demanded by the unusual surgery, he had thought of what to do with me afterwards. A proficient surgeon, he was also a profoundly decent man. *What more can I do than report his actions here?*

I was wheeled to a large bright hospital ward and hoisted gently onto the last bed on the left. My right leg was raised and suspended. Slowly my martyrized spirit returned to reality and I began to worry about the facts of day-to-day life. Would my identity card stand up to

Hitting Back

scrutiny? I had no ration card; how would I get ration stamps? Who should I inform? I noticed Walter Ardel standing by my bed. He had waited a long time, had not seen me, and decided to search for me in the hospital. Later that same day he brought me food stamps and informed the Organization. I slept long and deep. Unable to leave my bed, I was again faced with the problem of the bedpan.

By the next day, Friday, the bandage and the wrapped sheet were soaked with blood and pus and reeked horribly. The bandage was changed, but a few hours later the fresh bandage was also soaked through and equally malodorous. On Saturdays there was no doctor's round. I was nauseated by the repugnant, sweet, putrid smell of the pus and dried blood. After lunch I dozed, and while half asleep I heard somebody speaking to me. The nurse who had assisted at the operation was standing next to my bed together with two hospital porters holding a stretcher. My leg was gently lowered from the sling and I was carefully lifted onto the stretcher. A short time later I was lying on the table of the outpatients' surgery. My doctor appeared. He told the nurse what to fetch in order to clean the wound and change the bandage. She left the room and the doctor and I were alone for a few minutes. In a strained voice he told me that the Germans had announced that they would inspect the hospital. He deeply regretted that he could not let me stay on longer, despite my condition. He would attend to my wound as best he could, but then I would have to leave immediately. I noticed that my clothes were already prepared. He was quite subdued and did not find it easy to do what he had to. Obviously he believed I had accommodations, somewhere to stay when I left the hospital. I was very calm and sedate. I thanked him

In the Résistance

for all he had done. I didn't tell him that I had nowhere to go. This was not his concern.

The nurse arrived. She and the doctor worked quickly. The old bandage was removed and the wound thoroughly cleaned, but still pus seeped out. Gauze was stuffed into the wound, immediately soaked through and removed. This procedure was repeated two or three times and finally a long strip of gauze was left in the wound. Thick bandages were again applied, but this time without sheeting. The treatment was not pleasant, but while my leg was being seen to, I focused my thoughts on a different problem. Where would I go? What should I do? I had to make a decision. To return to the Colonel, Pierrette, and Françoise was impossible. If I turned up in this state, I would endanger the whole family and all the people hidden there. I would probably need further medical treatment. Can a doctor be let into the house? If so, what questions would he ask? I realized I couldn't go back there. A hotel? Limping and with a blood-soaked bandage, probably I would have been arrested on the first night. I knew a number of people in the Lyon Organization but only two or three of their addresses. Alex? Walter Ardel? I ruled out both since they lived in rented rooms. Who knew if they were at home? To turn up there would have involved them and put the police on their trail. Another option was an elderly couple, Michael (Michel) and Esther Kohn, who belonged to the Austrian group of the Lyon Organization that worked within the *Résistance*. They lived in a small village about ten kilometers outside Lyon. I had been there once before and as far as I knew they lived alone. Yes, that was a possibility.

The treatment was over and the bandage pressed tightly, as I presumed it was supposed to. I was helped into my clothes, and my *carte d'identité* and ration card were returned to me. I needed crutches. The nurse and the doctor shrugged with helplessness — after all, it was wartime and there weren't any available. I was helped down from the table but could stand only if I held onto something. The doctor handed me an old broomstick. It had been shortened for use as a makeshift walking stick. It had to do. The doctor performed yet another useful service for me: he ordered a taxi. I did not say this with irony; it was wartime and gasoline was scarce, but a hospital doctor had the authority to act so. It is ironic that the inconsequential aspects of normal everyday life, such as calling for a taxi, determined whether or not I would survive.

Supported by the nurse I got into the waiting taxi. It was Saturday evening and raining — not heavily, but enough to create a mood, like in films and novels where dramatic situations are invariably accompanied by rain. Two days ago, I had been operated on and ordered ten days of absolute rest. Now I was sitting in the back of a taxicab armed with a broomstick! I told the driver to take me to one of the bus stations in the outskirts of Lyon. From there I would take a bus to the Kohns. Not a single bus was standing at the terminal. Before I could ask the driver to check when the next bus to X would leave, he told me, "You won't have any luck today. The buses don't run on Saturday afternoon and Sunday because of the petrol shortage — *c'est la guerre.*" What now? I had told the driver that I had had an accident and since he had picked me up from the hospital he found that quite natural. "Can you drive me to "X," I asked, but he explained that his license was valid only for Lyon and he was not allowed to drive outside the city limits. "Sleep a night with relatives or friends in town," he advised

In the Résistance

good-naturedly. I again mentioned the accident, that my parents were worried and that I had to get home. He listened with growing impatience and repeated adamantly: "I am not allowed to drive you." I tried another tack: I told him how much money I had on me and that I was prepared to give it all to him as the fare, even though it was many times the normal tariff. This apparently soothed his conscience about breaking the license laws. We drove on.

As we approached the village I considered the implications of a car stopping at the Kohn's house late in the evening. Without doubt their first thought would be that the French or German police had come to round them up, which could elicit unforeseen reactions. I had to avoid that. Moreover, the taxi driver was not to know which house was my destination. That he knew which village was risky enough. We reached the village and I told the driver to stop. The roads were muddy and his car might get stuck. I paid him and he was glad to turn around and drive away. It was dark and still raining. I tried to orient myself. I calculated that it was about two hundred meters to the Skryabins's house. "Skryabin" was the Kohn's alias. What was two hundred meters? Not much of a distance, I think. Einstein knew better of course — it's all relative. After a few limping steps I realized I couldn't walk. I could stand on my left leg supported by the broomstick, but my right leg hung from my body like lead. Each attempt to put weight on my right leg sent pain shooting through my body. Perhaps I could hop on my left leg. I tried that but soon realized I would never manage two hundred meters. With no other alternative, I slipped to the ground and began to crawl. On all fours I made my way slowly, pausing every so often to rest. I was soaked through. It was not particularly warm but I sweated. The pain was fierce, but like a wounded animal I dragged myself on. I finally reached the house and knocked on the door. Esther opened the door and I greeted her. She recognized me and was shocked by my appearance, assuming that something terrible had happened. I pulled myself into the house and remained lying exhausted in the hall. Michel appeared, and Esther, an extremely practical woman, left only to return almost immediately with a towel, blankets, and a cup of hot tea. I recounted what had happened.

The Kohns, originally from Russia, where Michel was a member of the "Bund,"[8] lived in Vienna before coming to France. Here in Lyon they worked for the Austrian group within the M.O.I. (*Main d'Oeuvre Immigrée*) in the *Résistance*. Esther and Michel were in their mid-fifties; they were wise, intelligent, simple-living people, full of heart and feeling, always unselfish, always willing to help. Their own peace and safety was not their primary concern — helping others was. They looked like village folk and were quite indistinguishable from the local country people. Esther epitomized motherliness, which extended beyond her own children. You feel secure with her — cherished. She gave of herself completely, did more than seemed possible, quietly and without asking for thanks. She was also a fine cook and got much pleasure from seeing her food being enjoyed. It's a wonder how she managed to provide such food, after all it was the end of 1943. The war was in its fifth year and there was nothing to buy. But Esther was up and out at five o'clock every morning to hunt for milk, fruit, vegetables, eggs, and even meat from the farmers. She supplemented this with vegetables from her small garden. I will forever remember her *servietten-*

In the Résistance

knödel with *powidl,* a sweet dumpling with plum jam.

Esther removed my damp shoes and clothes, dried me off, poured tea into me, and took care of me as if I were a small sick child. Within a few minutes I was bedded on a sofa and tucked under blankets. Sounds from another room indicated that Esther, Michel, and I were not the only people in the house. Apparently two other comrades were also hidden there. It was my good fortune that I hadn't suspected that; had I known, I would never have dared to come to the Kohns for fear of leaving tracks for the police. Karl St. and Dr. Eva E. had been in hiding for a short time with Esther and Michel. They had belonged to a group of former volunteers from Austria, Germany, and Yugoslavia who had fought on the side of the Republicans against Franco's Fascists. They had been arrested by the Vichy police, charged with illegal subversive activities against the Germans and the Pétain government, found guilty, and imprisoned in the Castres fortress east of Toulouse. With the help of friends outside the group, they succeeded to escape in a daring, dramatic break-out. Two of them, Dr. E. and Karl St., found their way to Lyon and to the Kohns. How serendipitous — just when I needed medical attention there was a doctor under the same roof! Dr. E. tended to my open and still festering wound. But there was not much she could do in that setting.

It was time to change my quarters. Complications from the wound could lead to complications for all the occupants of the house. My friends in Lyon had been notified. They knew where I was and that I needed urgent medical care. Paul Kessler found a sanitarium where the doctor, nurses, and administrators were prepared to give me a bed without asking questions. That this alone was not enough will become apparent later. I took my leave of Michel and, above all, Esther. Despite the wound and the constant pain and in spite of the miserable circumstances, my stay with the "Skryabins" had been a comforting and comfortable interlude.

The Clinique Bon Abri ("Good Shelter" — *nomen est omen*) was not a hospital; it had none of the medical equipment usually associated with a clinic. The patients in the Clinique Bon Abri were not wounded, acutely ill, or awaiting surgery. I soon realized that most of the people here were elderly Jews who had gone underground and were waiting for the end of the war. I was allocated a bed in a double room; in the other bed was a Jew of about sixty years old, who had a severe nervous disorder. His whole body quivered uncontrollably. He was quite emaciated, yet ate enormous amounts of food. The doctor came each morning and the gauze drain in my wound was changed daily. The strips of gauze gradually became shorter as the wound closed from the inside. There was one particular nurse who had taken it upon herself to ensure that my nights were comfortable and not too long. Fortunately, my roommate was unaware of these nocturnal activities. Apart from my wound I am happy to say that I was a healthy twenty-five-year-old male.

It took another two weeks for the wound to close. I was sufficiently recovered to be able to leave the Clinique Bon Abri. I still limped a little but could cope with walking well enough. The Colonel was willing to take me in again, was even proud to do so, and a few days before Christmas I returned to my old room. The family had been very concerned and I had to describe at great length what had happened. They were all welcoming, particularly Pierrette and Françoise in their own special way. I was more attracted to Pierrette and a

In the Résistance

potentially sticky situation was resolved quickly. Pierrette and I got on very well. I was in contact with my friends but understandably couldn't do anything yet. It was Christmas time and I was thoroughly spoiled. Surprisingly, I felt a deep sense of contentment although the end of the war was not yet in sight. I spoke about what I wanted to do when the wound was healed completely, which I reckoned would be in two or three weeks. Pierrette wanted me to stay with them until the end of the war, perhaps afterwards too.

Confession

Meanwhile I spent time and effort getting used to my new self. I was now Alexandre Vasseur from Le Portel and I had all the documents to attest to my new identity. Since the bullet had been removed from my thigh, there was no evidence of a gunshot wound and I felt a lot safer.

On 30 December 1943, one day before the end of the year, my wound opened again and pus gushed out. We thought it was only superficial, most likely an infection of the scar, but the tugging in the muscle under the scar became stronger and the stream of pus continued. My temperature kept rising. Clearly it was more serious than a surface inflammation. My friends in Lyon did their best to find a doctor and a hospital where I could be thoroughly examined and everything necessary could be done. Through the mediation of French friends I was examined by a doctor at the Clinique Protestante of the Red Cross in Lyon. The diagnosis stated: after the first operation the wound was not properly tended, which resulted in the accumulation of suppurating fluid. A second operation was essential to reach the core of the infection.

With my new papers it was far easier to arrange a hospital appointment, albeit not without problems. In the middle of January 1944 I was admitted into the hospital and assigned to a surgical ward with twelve beds, all of them occupied. This time the operation was carried out properly—in an operating room and with a general anesthetic. Upon awakening, I felt the familiar wide and thick bandage. During rounds the doctor told

In the Résistance

me that they had had to cut deep into the center of the abscess that had developed. The wound could not be sutured and a pipe had been placed in the thigh to drain the pus. If asked I always gave the same answer. I had been involved in an accident and a sliver of metal had penetrated my thigh, which became infected and caused a pussy inflammation. No one had any reason to doubt this account. The other patients were occupied with their own aches, pains, and problems. One of them, a young man in his twenties, had been circumcised because of a constriction of his foreskin. The not inconsiderable discomfort he found in this condition was a constant source of amusement to the rest of us, particularly when he attempted to explain his problems to Sister Trotinette (we called the nun on our ward "Trotinette" because her brisk, firm footsteps could be heard from afar).

The finger-thick rubber piping was replaced by progressively narrower ones, until four weeks later only a few thin twisted strands of silk served to drain the last remnants of the abscess. There had been no particular calamities and it seemed to have gone well. Seemed! One day my temperature rapidly rose. The doctor was certain that the drains had been replaced too quickly and as a result the wound had closed around the abscess too soon, preventing the pus from draining out. He informed me that it was necessary to insert a larger drain to ensure that the welled-in pus could escape. Once the infection was cleared, the temperature would drop. A third operation? The doctor decided differently. A thin rubber pipe was attached to the silk threads leading through the flesh of my right thigh. This was pulled with force through the scarcely healed wound. The threads were now outside and the pipe inside. It did not take long, but I screamed from pain and was drenched in sweat. The nurse gave me an injection to calm me down. The diagnosis and therapy proved to be correct (although it could have been implemented a bit more gently, I thought) and my temperature dropped as more pus flowed out.

Despite its name, the Clinique Protestante did not treat only Protestants, Catholics were admitted, too, and all the nurses were nuns. In normal times a patient's religion was irrelevant, but 1944 — with the persecution and deportations of Jews a daily occurrence also in France — was a far cry from normal times. I had been in the hospital for almost two months. Soon it would be Lent and then Easter. I, Alexandre Vasseur, was not a Protestant, and therefore they deduced I must be a Catholic.

One of my childhood friends emigrated to Peru in 1938. On arrival he was asked by an immigration official: "Are you a Catholic?" When my friend answered that he was not, the official reacted with, "Ah, then you must be a Protestant." This status was entered into the records and from then on my friend in Peru was officially a Protestant. He told me this story when we met in Vienna in the 1960s.

A Catholic priest — a *curé* — periodically visited the Catholic patients, talking to them, praying with them, and taking confession. One day he approached me, asked how I was, where I came from, what I did, and tried to engage me in conversation. Then he wanted me to pray with him. The conversation had not bothered me at all, but I had a twofold, natural aversion to prayer: I was not religious or devout in any way and did not think much of the Jewish religious laws and regulations; neither did I relate to any other religion, and never had

In the Résistance

I even for a moment considered converting or improving my situation by entering another faith. I tried to lead the *curé* away from that path, digressed and made excuses. My claims that I had not attended church for a long time and no longer knew any of the prayers did not faze him, and he insisted that I fold my hands together and simply repeat his words. All eyes in the ward were fixed on me. There was nothing more dangerous for me than attracting attention. Why shouldn't Alexandre Vasseur quickly mumble a prayer to rid himself of the priest and of the other patients' attention? I clasped my hands together and uttered a few words of the prayer hesitantly and reluctantly. I interrupted abruptly and asked the priest if he could arrange for us to speak privately, alone. He was surprised. "I will try," he said and went off to discuss the arrangements with the nurse. Apparently he succeeded, for a short while later I was wheeled into a guest room where he was waiting. We were alone. I had the impression that the good man was waiting for a confession, the confession of a murderer. I didn't really know what I was doing or why. What could Alexandre Vasseur say to this priest without bringing more danger on himself? Caution and exposing nothing were the cardinal rules of living illegally. Any act of carelessness that might lead to questions regarding my borrowed identity could lead to disaster. I knew this only too well. Despite this, and against all reason, something inside me compelled me to react in a way for which I have no explanation. To his question about what I had on my mind, what it was I wanted to confess, I blurted out: "I did not say a prayer because I am Jewish. Please understand that I can act in no other way." No sooner did the words leave my mouth than I realized that I unnecessarily had placed myself in jeopardy. There was silence.

Hitting Back

On the face of the priest I could see, in turn, anger, disappointment, curiosity, and disbelief. What would he do? If he told anyone, I was lost. We stared at each other. I could not see my own expression, but he must have been able to read the fear in my eyes. Finally he broke the silence. "I am a little angry with you for not demanding to speak to me before you repeated the first words of the prayer. As you are Jewish, no doubt you are living in hiding. If you have any problems, either here in the hospital or after you are discharged, you can come to me and I will help you. I will give you my name and address." I breathed out and a great weight fell from my shoulders. Why did I do it? I didn't know. After the event there are many possible explanations. A devout Orthodox Jew later told me that I could have repeated the prayer without pangs of conscience; under the circumstances it would not have been a sin. He did not understand and I didn't bother explaining that I had not acted according to the criteria of what was a sin and what was not.

The healing process continued, the wound closed, and a scar formed. Finally, I was released from the hospital. "Finally," which suggests a welcome conclusion, is probably a misnomer in this context. I was actually trading protective walls, care, and a humane, friendly environment for the life of a hunted animal. But I could walk and, if necessary, run.

In the *Maquis*

It was the end of April 1944. Hitler's Germany and the Wehrmacht had already experienced many reverses, but, despite that, still occupied several countries, including France. The apparatus of terror, violence, and suppression still functioned and the destruction and extermination programs ran at full speed.

I was again at the disposal of the Lyon Organization and began looking for a room to rent. I settled in an attic room in a duplex not far from the Brotteaux station and the Rhône. It was well positioned and near a park. After negotiating the rent with the landlady (I appeared very serious and made a good impression on her) she said to me, "Monsieur, I hope I will have no problems with you. Your predecessor — a nice young man — was picked up by the Gestapo. His suitcase is still in the room." Evidently I had become quite hardened, as I took the room anyway. Two French students lived in the attic room across the hall from mine. After a short time we got to know more about each other. They noticed I had a book by Henri Barbusse and told me that they had studied for two semesters but were now fully involved with the F.F.I. (*Forces Françaises de l'Intérieur*). I enjoyed having people nearby who were my age and on the same wavelength.[9] On the other hand it was not ideal for my work and the security requirements it entailed. As for my Austrian friends, few were left in Lyon — some were back in Vienna and some had been arrested while sabotaging German property. I heard that Pit and Leo Trinczer had not survived.

One evening in May 1944 the man responsible for

Hitting Back

the Travail Allemand in southern France, "Lucien" (Oskar Grossmann), had a rendezvous with "P." at a tram terminal in Lyon. This tram line led to a German air force base. P. was a little late. The last tram of the day from the center of town arrived. This was usually filled with German soldiers who had quarters at the airfield or in a nearby barracks. Lucien waited near the tram stop. Soldiers were hanging on to the steps of the tram, singing and laughing. The tram stopped and a crowd of German soldiers of various rank spilled out. Suddenly there was a series of detonations. Hand grenades exploded, gunshots and machine gun barrages rang out. People were screaming, commands were shouted, more detonations followed. Because of the blackout it was totally dark. There was absolute pandemonium. In the dark it was impossible to estimate how many Germans were dead or wounded, but there were certainly many.

A troop of urban guerrillas had planned and carried out the ambush. They suffered no losses and escaped into the darkness. Lucien was hit in the eyes by grenade fragments and blinded instantly. He lay among the numerous uniformed victims, the only civilian. Ambulances and Red Cross vehicles arrived, gathering up the dead and injured, rushing them to hospitals. Only there did they notice the single civilian. Immediately he was under suspicion of having been involved in the ambush, and a search of his clothing revealed items of great interest to the Gestapo.

We knew what had happened at the terminal and that Lucien had fallen into the hands of the Nazis. Other details were filled in bit by bit. The German occupying force was incensed: police raids were conducted continually; there were public executions; the deportations of young people to Germany increased. In rapid

In the Résistance

succession comrades were arrested — in Lyon, Limoges, Toulouse, and, especially, Paris and Vienna. A major part of the network of the Austrian resistance organization within the M.O.I. and in Vienna itself was destroyed. We had to act quickly to save whatever could be saved. I assumed responsibility for regrouping, changing of accommodations, and assigning new identities to comrades who, until now, were not yet targeted. I was permanently on the move and had perfected avoiding the police. I could smell them from afar. This was just as well, since I was almost never "clean" and frequently carried false documents for my comrades.

Alex, who belonged to a group of urban guerrillas, gave me the address of Walter Ardel. He felt that something was wrong there. I had had this experience before and paid for it dearly. Of course I should not have gone — but how could I not after all that Walter Ardel had done for me?

I rang the bell to his apartment and a pleasant-looking woman of about fifty opened the door a crack. Softly I asked for Walter. The woman examined me and asked quickly, "Are you a friend?" "Yes," I answered. "Please leave immediately. Monsieur Walter was fetched this morning." My legs turned to lead and I walked away as quickly as I could. We later learned that Walter was tortured and deported. He did not survive.[10]

Faces and images flood my mind. I jot down fragmented memories and by doing so am acutely conscious that I am alive. So many times I stood on the edge and the unavoidable passed me by. Others survived too, certainly, but why did I?

What had happened? Through Lucien's unfortunate accident a list of names fell into the hands of the

Hitting Back

Gestapo: cover names, nicknames, and *noms de guerre*. Some of the names led to the conclusion that they belonged to former Austrians. A special commando of the Gestapo — made up of Austrian officers — was formed, working partially in Vienna and partially in Lyon and Paris. Research in Vienna revealed the same cover names in the files of people who were known to be Communists and revolutionary Socialists. I should mention that my name "Dolly" was also on the list, but again I was lucky: "Dolly" suggested a girl's name and was not listed in any file or card index.

What was skillfully disguised for years had been unmasked. Lucien was blind and lay closely guarded in a single room in a Lyon hospital. Since he could not see, he was fully dependent on the spoken word. Some Viennese Gestapo people who knew the political scene in Vienna before 1938 arrived in Lyon with a special plan: they visited Lucien, posing as friends, comrades, and colleagues. For hours on end they sat at his bedside and talked about the "work" of the "Organization," at the same time mentioning the nicknames of friends. In this way they pumped information from Lucien that led to the arrest and death of many. It was a satanic plan conceived by devils. When they could get nothing more out of him, his life was meaningless to them and he was murdered. Lucien could not have continued living had he known what he had done in good faith. Only one person in Vienna escaped arrest and deportation. Egon Kodicek was fortunate that news of him had not yet reached Vienna from Lyon. Had Lucien not vetoed my return to Vienna the previous year, I would have suffered the same fate as the others on the list.

It was no longer possible to continue working as before. A new period had begun and we had to rethink.

In the Résistance

Together with Otto B., a friend from Vienna, I decided to join a partisan unit. We went to the *maquis*. I knew Otto and his brother from Vienna, where they had also lived in the ninth district. Otto's brother was deported in 1942 and died in a concentration camp. Following advice from our friends in the M.O.I., we decided to join a group operating in Ardèche. Within the F.N. (*Front National*) and the F.F.I. there was a wide array of groups inside the *Résistance* and among the partisans. The range stretched from the Gaullists to the Communists. Not surprisingly, there were great differences of opinion about immediate objectives. But irrespective of how the battle should be fought, all the groups were united in a single goal: free France from German occupation. Unfortunately that was about the only point of agreement. There were two principal lines of thought:

> *Readiness* — wait until the American and British armies reached France and then, with the Free French under the leadership of Charles De Gaulle, join up with Gaullist troops.
>
> *Action* — practice active resistance, i.e., constant attacks, dealing the Germans smaller and larger blows in order to demoralize the German soldiers, free some regions, frighten the collaborators, neutralize them and thus prepare for the total defeat of the Nazi army.

Among the various partisan units were the A.S. (*Armée Secrète*), *La France d'abord,* and the F.T.P.F. (*Franc-Tireurs et Partisans Français*). The M.O.I. worked, for the most part, together with groups of the F.T.P.F. This mini-description of the political scene, albeit incomplete, perhaps helps to explain the situation at that time.

Otto and I set off. The distance from Lyon to Valence down the Rhône valley is about a hundred kilometers.

Hitting Back

But in order to avoid the main roads we had to make several detours and travel almost 150 kilometers. A truck gave us a lift and let us off about forty kilometers into the region of Vienne. We were on the east side of the Rhône. We marched along village lanes and footpaths and spent the first night in an open field. Naturally we had left Lyon without any luggage. Apart from what I was wearing, everything I owned remained in my rented room, which, of course, I left without informing my landlady. We continued the next day, partially by foot, sometimes hopping on farm carts for a short way. The region east of the Rhône was flatter and less densely populated than that on the west bank. The closer we got to the legendary Vercors and to the Ardèche the clearer it became that the Germans were no longer the undisputed masters of France. The Vercors, which lies between the *départements* of Drôme and Isère, was controlled by the partisans. The German army, supported by special units, periodically undertook massive "cleaning" operations, but despite these the Vercors remained under the control of the partisans. As early as June 1944 the Germans had restricted themselves to holding the larger towns, the main roads, the railway lines, and the main lines of communication. The mountains and the woods were in the hands of the partisans. The same was true of Ardèche.

We spent the following night in a farmhouse somewhere between Valence and Die. It was no secret to the farmer that we were heading for the *maquis*, so we spoke openly. We were well cared for and he promised to take us into Ardèche. The only problem was that we had to cross the Rhône and the bridges over the Rhône were guarded. We had to reckon on checkpoints and that our papers would be examined. In clothing lent to us by

In the Résistance

the farmer we looked like country workers. He took us with him in his truck, ostensibly to fetch pigs for slaughter. He had brought wine and parcels of meat for the border guards.

At the bridge the guards looked into the back to check for weapons. They waved us on. We didn't imagine it would be so easy. We were in Ardèche! The farmer dropped us off about ten kilometers into the region, somewhere near Privas. We thanked him and walked on. But where to go? "To the *maquis*" was easy to say, but it had no address, no street name, no number. The area was vast and the wooded hills and mountains ranged between 600 and 1500 meters high. Somewhere, no doubt, we would come across people, perhaps farmers or even partisans, whom we could ask. We felt fairly safe. We walked and greeted passers-by, who returned our greeting. We approached a man who seemed trustworthy and asked him where we should go. He took us to an inn where we had a long conversation. The same evening we were taken to an area that was used by several military underground organizations for training and as operational headquarters. Just about everyone was French. From the beginning we had made no secret of the fact that we were "Autrichiens" (not Germans) and were living with French documents under assumed names. We stayed for a week, received training in the handling of weapons, and took part in combat exercises. Considering us adequately trained, the commander allocated us to a battalion of the F.T.P.F. in which the M.O.I. was strongly represented. Upon our departure a comrade presented me with a large drum revolver and ammunition.

We were now southwest of Valence. The group we wanted to join operated in an area that was about fifty

Hitting Back

kilometers further in the direction of Lyon. We continued our journey partially by car and partially on foot. We reported to Commander Lieutenant "Basile" in St. Félicien near Tournon. We were accepted and allowed to stay. The unit lived in primitive hay barns, wooden huts, and tents. The commander and a few others occupied an abandoned building. Our daily routine consisted of exercises, weapons training, and map reading, in short, an accelerated type of military training tailored for partisan warfare. Our equipment and weaponry were inadequate and of poor quality. We were a colorful bunch; there was no single uniform although the British army jackets (khaki shirts) and caps were at least the same. The battalion was about 110 men strong and, with few exceptions, was made up of youths, two-thirds of whom were French. They came from Tournon, Valence, Vienne, and nearby. The rest were immigrants who had been living in France for varying lengths of time — Poles, Yugoslavs, Spaniards, Bulgarians, Czechs, one German, and Otto and I, two Austrians. Additional weapons were acquired by attacking single German soldiers or small groups. In an attack on a train at a small railway station we captured, among other things, machine guns, hand grenades, German uniforms, and a mortar. The information for the attack had come from the local people. Frequently we had to get our food in the same way. Some of our food was given to us by farmers voluntarily, some of it we requisitioned. In each case the farmers were given receipts so that they could demand compensation from a free French government after the war. We had plenty of time to sit together and talk. Not far from us were military groups belonging to the *Armée Secrète* and a battalion of *La France d'abord*. Both these units were well provided for by the Allies through various

In the Résistance

channels. The *Armée Secrète*, in particular, received weapons, uniforms, and other equipment from parachute drops and had more than they needed. They also had radio contact. However, all attempts to get weapons from or through them failed. They considered themselves the elite and even condemned our military activities.

The war continued. This was the first time I had ever used a weapon. There was shooting and killing too. How different it was from my previous activities, like in the *zone interdite*! Here I was not alone. I felt far stronger morally and more secure and I didn't need to watch my every word. My identity card no longer had any meaning. I was who I really was. Everyone here knew that I was Jewish and Austrian, and they called me by my nickname "Dolly." In my case "Dolly" was my *nom de guerre*. I still have an identity card in my possession today — a piece of paper, about 3 x 6 cm, with the stamp of the F.T.P.F. and the name "Dolly" clearly legible on it. This piece of paper was at that time as useful as a passport is today.

This document served like a passport.

Fighting in Tournon

By July 1944 we knew that the Germans had already lost the war, but they were still present as an occupying force, were supported by French collaborators, had a well-equipped army, and could still carry out counter-offensives. They were still murderers who were to be taken seriously. I and most of the others in the battalion — a wild bunch of young people with neither war nor military experience, poorly equipped with primitive weapons — acted as if the German army no longer existed. Whether justified or not, we were confident. We were correct inasmuch as the Germans avoided the hills and the woods, wrong insofar as they repeatedly combed certain areas and massacred everyone they found. The atmosphere in our unit must have been similar to that in the other partisan groups. I learned to use a rifle, a machine gun, a pistol, and hand grenades. I had no doubt that it was necessary, but I had no innate feeling for weapons and knew that I never would. The training was intensive and we were sure it would soon be put to use.

In the meantime the war followed its course. In June 1944 the Allies successfully landed at Cherbourg and St. Lô. Caen was attacked on July 9th and conquered, despite heavy losses. On July 20 an assassination attempt on Hitler by German officers failed and Himmler took command of the army.[11] In a massive offensive the Soviet troops drove the Germans out of vast areas of Russia, advanced into the Baltic states, and by August reached Poland, Sofia, Bucharest, and Budapest. On August 1 the British and American armies created the long-

In the Résistance

awaited "second front" in Brittany, and were actively supported by the forces of the French *Résistance*. On August 20 the American troops had Paris under siege, and the German occupation forces surrendered on August 25, following an insurrection led by the *Résistance*. At the beginning of August we set out to liberate Tournon.

For this mission we descended during the night. Part of our battalion and some heavy weaponry with ammunition were to be taken by truck as close to the road as possible but remain screened in the woods. The unit was split up into small groups, some of only two or three men. Watches, as far as these existed, were coordinated and precisely set. We made our way down the mountain, through woods and fields, in socks or barefooted, with our shoes slung over our shoulders to avoid making any sound. We approached Tournon in wide, extended order. At exactly 4 A.M. we opened fire using all our weaponry. Our specific targets were the bridge, the military barracks, and the commander's office; the final objective was to block the streets and occupy the railway station.

Our attack went according to plan. Two comrades and I were assigned to destroy a German machine gun emplacement. With machine guns and hand grenades we inched our way forward to the camouflaged emplacement. We managed to get close enough to lob the hand grenades. A few minutes elapsed and the machine gun remained silent. One German soldier had been badly wounded, a second soldier came towards us with his hands raised in surrender. Both were shot dead. I noticed that I had no idea what the others were doing, where they were, who was in front and who behind us. We searched the nearby houses for German soldiers. Shots

Hitting Back

rang out continuously but who was shooting at whom? We turned around and went off in the direction of the barracks and the bridge. In one house we found three Germans who were quartered there. They shivered with fear, gave up their weapons voluntarily, and allowed themselves to be bound. They walked in front of us — prisoners and human shields against bullets.

At around 8 A.M. all was still. The objective of the attack had been accomplished. The Germans, already lacking confidence, greatly overestimated our strength in numbers and weaponry. Moreover, we had surprised them, while, except for a few sentries, they were sleeping. In panic they fled as far as they could over the Rhône bridge. Many German soldiers were killed. The picture in and around the barracks was a disaster for the Germans. The losses in our battalion, dead or wounded, were minimal. Tournon was liberated and we remained there for about two weeks. We still had to be cautious, particularly at night, because the Germans were still on the other side of the Rhône and were shooting at us with heavy artillery.

I should have been satisfied that I was finally participating actively in killing the hated Nazi soldiers and their officers and witnessing the carnage. Far from it. I was anything but satisfied. What was wrong with me? Had I not waited anxiously for this day? Had I not made every effort to achieve this? Yes, and no. For me, the battle against suppression, against mass murder and its perpetrators, was not the same as hunting hares. I knew very well that the battle against injustice, oppression, racism, and even genocide, could not be won with words. And without question, to appeal to the mercy of the murderers or instigators who issued the orders, by asking them politely to stop, would be in vain. The ratio-

In the Résistance

nale for my actions was not to kill Nazis — who represent the most perfect machinery of murder — but to participate in the dawn of an era in which humankind did not murder at all. In contrast, the primary motivation of the battalion was somewhat different. The battalion consisted of young Frenchmen from Tournon and its surroundings. They were in touch with their families and friends, and, as heroes of the moment, allowed themselves to be honored. Killing had not been their craft. But they were determined to drive out the Germans and that could not be achieved without killing. A successful mission like this one gave them a sense of satisfaction.

We had been in Tournon for almost two weeks, when we learned that German units with tanks were moving up along the Rhône from Marseille. Lieutenant Basile ordered us to return to our old quarters immediately. We had no choice but to leave Tournon at once. Soon afterwards we heard that American troops that were already in Cannes had united with troops of the Free French in Toulon and Marseille and were pushing together up the Rhône valley in the direction of Lyon. The retreating German units passed through Tournon. Three days later we liberated Tournon from the departing German troops a second and final time. The regular Free French army and American troops had not yet arrived. But during the three days that the retreating German units were in Tournon they searched for people who had given shelter or support to the partisans. In that short time they rampaged among the civilian population, shooting dozens of men and women. They carried out their murders in public places and left the dead where they lay. The people they killed were the mothers, fathers, relatives and friends of our French comrades. In response, every German soldier that fell into the hands of my comrades was immediately killed. Can I, can anybody blame them? Hardly. The direct, personal experience was so emotionally overwhelming that I classify it as normal behavior. Prisoners were taken. Lieutenant Basile had more than a few of them executed. Otto B. and I refused to join these execution commandos. We did not even have to disobey orders; we simply did not volunteer.

During this time I met another man from Vienna, Kurt Armand. He was one of our group, also within the M.O.I., and the commander of a partisan unit operating in the vicinity of Nimes. He came to Tournon with some of his people to join up with the French-American army in their push to Lyon. Lyon was liberated in the first days of September 1944.

But this "victory" and the sense of elation that followed soon lost its gleam for Otto B. and me, as we found ourselves once again victims. Lieutenant Basile had established his headquarters, the *quartier général*, with some of his recruits on the main square of Tournon, and the others, including us, moved into the barracks. Lieutenant Basile's intention was to strengthen the core of our battalion, join up with the French troops who were pushing up towards Metz, and fight alongside them until the whole of France was liberated or the war ended. Basile's new unit, however, admitted only Frenchmen. Somebody must have told him — I can't imagine why — that Otto B. and I were German spies. We had been in Tournon for just a few days when Basile had us summoned. This took the form of four armed comrades escorting us to headquarters. Basile took us into a room that looked onto a courtyard. He and another of our superiors played court martial (I use the word "played"

In the Résistance

but it could have had appalling consequences). They accused us of being German spies and having wormed our way into the unit with subversive intentions. They began the interrogation by waving a loaded pistol that they threatened to use. Otto B. could speak very little French and the little he could utter was in a hard Viennese accent. I was the defendant for both of us. The two prosecutors screamed at us. On the outside we remained quite calm and I answered cautiously. I had the feeling that neither Basile nor his colleague felt at ease in his role. After all, it was one thing to shoot the enemy — whether German soldiers or French collaborators — but two comrades who had fought alongside them in their battalion? That was something else. It was a grotesque and ghastly situation. Basile claimed that the clearest evidence that we were spies and that I was lying was my pale and sweaty face. My retort was terse but it caused a turnabout. I asked Basile how his face would look were he the one being accused and threatened by a gun-toting comrade. In addition, I maintained (which was true) that we were all sweating because the room was stuffy and hot. He calmed down and exchanged a few words with his subordinate. They put their pistols away. Basile ordered us to return to the barracks, pack our personal belongings, and leave Tournon.

Thus we left the *quartier général*. All the comrades who had witnessed the scene — they asked us for all the details of the interrogation — were on our side. We didn't have much to take from our lockers in the barracks. We returned the weapons we had been given to the office and were given receipts. We were also given documents verifying the time we had spent with the battalion. I stuck the heavy barreled revolver I had brought with me to the battalion visibly into my belt.

Hitting Back

We had not gone far and were still within the town limits when two comrades on motorcycles caught up with us. On the orders of the commander, we were to return immediately to headquarters. Almost the entire battalion and many of the townspeople stood outside the *quartier général* in a jagged semi-circle. Basile had planted himself theatrically in front of the door of the headquarters. We had to step in front of him with the circle of onlookers behind us. In clipped sentences he again accused us, announcing that he would have us executed for stealing vital military property from the limited resources of the French army. He meant that we had not returned the weapons that belonged to the battalion. Without doubt there must have been a few people in our battalion who had it in for Otto and me — as Austrians or Germans — and wanted to cause us harm. We were lucky that the accusation was dramatized in such a scene in front of everyone. We presented our receipts proving that we had returned our army property. Everyone knew that my barrel revolver was my own property and did not come from their military storage area.

And that was that. Whoever wanted to harm us had failed and Basile had exposed himself to ridicule. He ordered us to leave Tournon immediately and that as of 6 P.M. we were to be considered outlaws. If anyone saw us in Tournon after the stroke of six, he had license to shoot us. It was midday and within the hour Tournon lay behind us.

Basile was not a bad or evil man, but a small lieutenant (in stature too) who had become the hero of the day. Ensconced in his roomy *quartier général*, the "liberator" of Tournon knew that everyone wanted something from him. The war was still not over and the out-

In the Résistance

come on the fronts still not clear. It was a confusing scenario of German prisoners, scattered German soldiers, fleeing Germans in uniform and civilian clothing, former and present collaborators, partisans of all hues, re-formed French army units, and American troops. Victims of the occupation and the Pétain regime wanted the guilty to be punished, but the guilty — as was their ilk — shouted "stop the thief" and accused the innocent. Greater men than Basile could not have coped with the situation. He let us go and we survived. I cannot reproach him.

The document attesting to our service in Basile's regiment.

Liberated France

Otto and I, peaceful but wild-looking companions, walked to Lyon, which had already been liberated. All we had to do was meet friends from our group in the Rue Paul Bert. I still had things in my last lodgings and could now go there with confidence instead of anxiety. To be free and no longer persecuted was something entirely new and took some getting used to, as did walking with a straight back and being able to talk with friends in public. The transition was quick but the years of persecution and humiliation were never shrugged off completely.

The Austrians in the French *Résistance* thought of returning to Vienna, Vienna in a free and newly constituted Austria. It was not possible yet, but it was no longer a dream. As before, we did not want to wait to see what, if anything, others would do for us. The chimneys of the destruction factories were still belching out smoke and the mass murder in the concentration camps continued. Nazi propaganda now had a new theme: the "Wuwa" (*Wunderwaffe*), the wonder weapon that reportedly had the capacity to annihilate everything in its wake. Hundreds of thousands were still dying at the front. Could we not at least celebrate our own re-won freedom, enjoy the sun, and let things take their course? But we just could not let go and felt compelled to carry on the fight.

With the agreement of the M.O.I. and the French authorities of the liberated regions we decided to make contact with the Austrians in the prisoner-of-war camps. We were to discuss the repugnant Nazi war with them,

In the Résistance

form anti-Fascist committees with them, and strengthen their consciousness of being Austrians rather than *Ostmärker* or Germans. Equipped with documents to gain entry into the prisoner-of-war camps, I travelled to Grenoble. The indelible impression left on me by Grenoble that first evening was not so much its beauty as the light emanating from it. After the many years of darkness from the blackouts imposed on towns to avoid enemy bombing, I saw and physically felt a brightly lit town again for the first time. I walked through the streets and enjoyed the sense of light on my body like a cool shower on a hot summer evening. I literally bathed in the light. I have never since been back to Grenoble, but whenever I hear or think of it I associate it with light and brightness. I would like to return there one day.

Despite my letter of reference and the documents I had from Lyon it was difficult to obtain entrance into the prison camp. I had to get past distrust, bureaucracy, and rejection. Neither the French army nor the authorities understood what I wanted. Their mistrust would have filled me with fear had I less experience behind me. In the prisoner-of-war camps I had to deal with German officers who behaved like they were still the masters of the world, but my sharp reprimands in their own language subdued them. I soon learned, however, not to try and enter any camp after dark; both the German occupants and the French guards were hostile and it could be dangerous.[12]

Many Nazis, from the SS, the Gestapo, and German army officers, had fled into neighboring Switzerland. They were all taken in by the "good" Swiss. I did not know of a single instance of fleeing Nazis being returned to the border and handed over to the French authorities, as the Swiss had done with refugees from 1938 to 1943.

Hitting Back

During my sojourn in Grenoble I had a heart-warming chance encounter. I was sitting in a bistro with a number of people and we were talking about the war, the successes on the various fronts, the unsatisfactory provision of food, and the prospect of peace. I spoke about my activities and somebody asked me:

"Are you Austrian?"

"Yes," I replied, "and you?"

"Also," he said. "Are you Viennese?" he asked further.

"Yes," I replied again, "and you?"

"I lived in Wiener Neustadt."

"Interesting," I said, "I was born in Wiener Neustadt."

"Is your name Irving perhaps?" he asked.

"No, I am Dolly."

It was Max Schlinger. His family had had a shop in Wiener Neustadt selling bicycles and sewing machines. They were friends of my parents and Max was about the same age as my brother Irving. We talked about old times and future plans well into the night.

The work with the prisoners was not at all productive and I decided to return to Lyon. In order to make contact with the center of our organization I travelled to Paris by train with Leo Z. and Kurt Armand. This time it was no cattle car but a comfortable compartment. The weather was good and we enjoyed the view through the open window. We talked, laughed, read, smoked, and behaved like normal people. Paris! Free and liberated Paris! Paris, the city in which the *Résistance* forced the German army to capitulate. Paris, which the Germans wanted to destroy with their "burnt earth policy" but failed thanks to the efforts of the F.F.I. This vital, pulsating metropolis had lost much of its power but it had

In the Résistance

not been broken. It was my birthday, and seeing this city and being able to experience it again was a perfect birthday gift.

While I was in Paris, Belgrade was liberated. Tito and his army of partisans were recognized by the Allies. They were prepared to repatriate Yugoslav citizens. Himmler recruited the *Volkssturm* — children and old men who were called up and sent to the front as cannon fodder. The Nazis had now become murderers of their own people. We discussed ways in which we could participate in the battle for the total annihilation of a Fascist Germany and the liberation of Austria. There were not too many of us left. Our clandestine war had cost many lives. Even in the last weeks and days before the liberation of many regions of France numerous friends were arrested by the Gestapo and sent to concentration camps where they died. The group of Austrians (Communists, former Social Democrats, sympathizers of no specific party, young girls and youths — and even a few Germans) that had actively fought with the French *Résistance* and the *Front National* was largely decimated.[13] The survivors, I among them, decided to go to Yugoslavia to join up with Marshall Tito's partisan army, and — as Austrians — help in the liberation of Austria.

Meanwhile, I returned to Lyon. Pierrette was waiting for me, and I spent carefree weeks and unforgettable days and nights there. But the newspapers, the radio, conversations, discussions, and the small food rations, made it impossible to ignore the realities of the war and the hardships of everyday life. To me, however, everything seemed so easy, so simple, anything was possible. Liberation had reached not only parts of France, not just Lyon and Paris: I too had been liberated, freed from an enormous pressure that had weighed me down

Hitting Back

for so long. Everything had a different quality — the meetings and the rendezvous, the girls, the parks, the squares, the bistros, the streets, the walks, even the air. I realized that I too had changed. My life would have been considerably poorer had I not experienced that special time, from October to December 1944. Could a few weeks compensate for all those years? Most people, I believe, would argue that irrespective of the duration of the good times in their lives, it is the difficult, the terrible, the painful times that have the greater impact. But I didn't see it that way. I chose to be optimistic and to dream, yet I remained with both feet planted on *terra firma*. I spent a lot of time with my friends, talking about the flood of news, both good and bad.

The Soviet army daily liberated new regions and more towns. The Allies were now in Belgium and France, close to the German border. But in the middle of December the German army began its counteroffensive in the Ardennes. German propaganda maximized the army's successes, painting (from our point of view) horrific pictures. The Americans were not used to such stiff resistance. Some of the collaborators became active again. The outcome was still not clear and many questions remained unanswered. Were the fronts rolling back? Did Hitler really have a "wonder weapon?" Would this war ever end? Many people lived again in fear. I had not yet contacted Mama or my brother and sister. They knew nothing of me and I nothing of them. When I saw my brother again at the end of 1945, I discovered that he had landed with the American troops in France and had served as a staff sergeant in the fierce battle in the Ardennes.

Finally, the opportunity to go to Yugoslavia presented itself. It was time to say goodbye to Pierrette and

In the Résistance

to Lyon. It wasn't easy to tear myself away. A group of young Austrians had come from Belgium, some from the security of Switzerland, and together with friends from Lyon we travelled to Marseille. I still had a *carte d'identité* with a false name and could stroll through the city of Marseille along the Canebière, its artery. The docks had been blown up for the most part but the bars around the harbor were all open. For the bar owners, the girls and their pimps, it was immaterial whether the clients were French, German, American, white or black, as long as there was money, cigarettes, and other items, including certain luxuries that otherwise could be bought only on the black market.

Only a few people were informed as to how and when we could board a troop carrier. Although Yugoslavia already had official representation in Marseille, agreements with them lay beyond the area of jurisdiction allowed by the Allies. There were not many of us left after the years of persecution, the camps and prisons, the periods of active underground, and the many waves of arrests. It was decided that the older men, women, and girls could not go with us to Yugoslavia, as they would no doubt be turned back by the authorities. That left barely twenty of us. I was now twenty-six, some were younger. Our point of departure was a house on the outskirts of the city, belonging to an Austrian friend, Harry S., who lived there with his wife and child. Harry was active in the *Résistance* in the region of Marseille, and after the liberation had gotten to know some people in the new civilian administration and the French military. Since his wife was American (they had met during the Spanish Civil War) he also knew many Americans. The family had moved into the large house only after the liberation of Marseille.[14]

Hitting Back

Around Christmas 1944 we were told to board a British ship. Since our only chance of joining the ship was to pose as Yugoslavs, we agreed to leave all our documents with Harry and to pass through the control points without any papers. We had to report to a British-Yugoslav commission in a building at the harbor. Each of us received a number corresponding to a list held by the Yugoslav representative on the commission. My number was 331, which I had to be able to say in Serbo-Croat: *tristotridisatadin*. I knew no other word in that language, nothing about Yugoslavia, and the others were no better. To reach the harbor from Harry's house we had to cross the city. We travelled in two groups by tram. About ten of us, including myself, stood on the rear, open car of the tram. Our spirits were high. After a few stops the tram remained standing longer than usual, and a few minutes later we were surrounded by police and civilians who were openly hostile towards us. What was wrong? Only later did we learn what had happened that Christmas in 1944. The German Ardennes offensive in the direction of Antwerp was at its height. The newspapers and radio were reporting daily that German parachutists were jumping behind Allied lines. Rumors supplemented the news. The population of the liberated regions had been warned and an appeal for caution was broadcast.

We, of course, were immediately suspect. But we were no longer afraid of the Germans and were guileless towards the French. We acted like yokels. Our young Belgian friends were not shy to speak German; others spoke French with a strong accent. All of us had our belongings in bags or small cases. One of the Belgians had a backpack from Vienna, visibly carried a Zeiss camera, and was wearing knee socks and hiking

In the Résistance

shoes. We obviously appeared suspicious. In fact, we were lucky we weren't lynched. As soon as the police made us leave the tram they demanded our documents. None of us, of course, had any papers. Our jocular attitude had obviously raised their hackles and they weren't at all amused. With their whistles they summoned reinforcements and escorted us to the police station. What could we possibly tell them to explain our situation? Our behavior was exceedingly stupid, provocative, perhaps even dangerous.

At the police station they searched our luggage. In my bag they found the barrel revolver with ammunition from my time with the partisans. Two others also had weapons. Almost all of us had military water bottles. Without question the police considered us to be German parachutists and we were interrogated individually. They did not believe a word we said. The evidence spoke out against us: military water bottles, weapons, a Zeiss camera, and no documents. Moritz Fels-Margulies was persistent and demanded to speak to the chief superintendent. Finally they agreed and Moritz attempted logically to explain to the officer the improbability of our situation. He also requested that the officer telephone the Yugoslav consul or the responsible Yugoslav representative. The chief superintendent phoned but there was no answer. No one was in the office. Only later did we understand how fortuitous that was. Had the Yugoslav representative answered the phone, he would have had to deny knowledge of us. Officially he could not acknowledge our existence and naturally would sacrifice us before endangering an entire transport. The interrogations lasted a few hours. Luckily Moritz knew the mayor of Marseille, who was a Communist and who had a leading role in the *Résis-*

tance.[15] The chief superintendent spoke with the mayor. We were nervous and tired.

The scene then changed dramatically and took on a comic twist. Moritz was still in the chief superintendent's office. Harry S. entered the room in which we were sitting guarded by the police. He was holding a bundle of all possible (and impossible) documents with various stamps on them. He gave one of the documents to the first *flic* he saw, and, without even looking at the policeman, turned to us and said, "You can go." Things moved very quickly. Harry, who knew the people from the *Résistance* in Marseille, was soon speaking with the chief superintendent. The latter had problems explaining to his people that we were not enemies or German parachutists, but Slovenians simply trying to return home.

In the evening we made our way to the harbor. Reciting our numbers instead of names was enough to get through the checkpoint and we were allocated tents to sleep in. A weight was lifted from our minds. All we had to deal with was the cold. Although Marseille was in the south of France, between Christmas and New Year of 1944 an ice-cold wind blew in the night. Some of us were on camp beds, others had to lie on the floor. We had no blankets and we woke up in the morning stiff from the cold. On our third evening in port, a British troop carrier docked, took us on board, and set sail the same evening.

The Road to Austria

It was my first time at sea. I had no idea how large or powerful a steamer is. There were German prisoners of war in the hold below. Yugoslavs (or those posing as such) were accommodated between decks. I was in the recreation room with about forty people; the room was full to bursting. Every available surface, including tables and benches, was occupied, and from the ceiling hammocks were suspended one next to the other. It was stuffy and the whole ship reeked. I was sweating, while just a few hours earlier I had been freezing. The ship set sail for Italy. We were to land at Bari. Between Corsica and Sardinia we were hit by a violent storm and the ship rolled and twisted. Few on board had sea legs or sailing experience, and most of the passengers looked green. They vomited in the recreation rooms, in the corridors, on the staircases, and on deck. Whoever was able to restrain himself considered himself a hero. I tried to get over the worst of it with the usual black humor but my stomach and innards rebelled. Unable to hold it any longer, I rushed out of the recreation room, getting as far as the iron staircase. What I encountered there defies description. The contents of my stomach mixed with the spewed-out contents of others. I held onto the railing so I wouldn't slip over, and, with effort, succeeded to climb the slippery steps up to the deck.

The air was better there but the floor was awash with green slime. The swaying of the ship made me dizzy and the foul stench prompted my stomach to eject its last contents and bile. A modicum of delicacy drove me to the railing to spew into the sea and not onto the gang-

Hitting Back

plank. My feet had no grip and I had no power in my legs. It was like standing on an ice rink. Waves pounded and partially flooded the deck. The ship suddenly dipped, another large wave crashed onto the deck, and I lost my grip on the railing. Moritz was nearby; he grabbed me and tossed me onto a coil of ropes. I landed with my rear end in the center of the ropes as if in a funnel, with my head and feet hanging over the sides. My hands were pressed against my stomach. I would probably have fallen overboard had it not been for Moritz.

The storm died down. Everyone was occupied with cleaning the ship and their clothing, but the stench remained. Corsica from a distance was beautiful and wild, but all I could think of was the severity of the storm. The Costa Smeralda on Sardinia was breathtaking, but my memories of Sardinia have a greenish tinge that has nothing to do with the green of emeralds.

The journey took us further through the Straits of Messina. Our sense of fun returned and we played the clown: we untied the strings of the hammocks holding our friends so that they fell to the floor—fortunately the storm had not dissipated their sense of humor. We expected to disembark in Bari, but for some reason the ship docked in Taranto. From there we travelled by truck to Bari, where we were taken to a collection camp. Would I ever see the end of collection camps? But we could come and go as we pleased and I wandered through the streets. Curiously there were no pavements, which seemed to signify pedestrians were not welcome. To pass the time in the camp Otto and I played *zensern*, a card game that was popular in Budapest and Vienna. It was damp and cold and very unpleasant. To amuse myself and others I put snow in the beds of those who were particularly sensitive, while they were

In the Résistance

sleeping. Their reaction was quite predictable and despite their annoyance we all had a good laugh. We did not stay long in the camp. One day we were picked up in trucks and told we would be traveling to Yugoslavia by plane. The truck stopped in front of the aerodrome and we sat inside and waited, freezing. Three hours later we returned to the camp without any explanation. Apparently, due to a misunderstanding, the American military authorities did not allow the plane to take off. But the following day everything went according to plan. We boarded a twin-propeller plane, sitting on benches along its fuselage. We were given parachutes and an explanation of how to use them. The plane did not fly very high — it was not the type that did — and it was cold during the flight. I had no fear of flying and was not at all nervous. The flight passed well for all of us and we landed in Belgrade without complications. My virgin sea voyage had been followed a few days later by my virgin air flight; I felt quite the seasoned traveler.

At the beginning of January 1945 we were lodged in the Hotel Moskwa in Belgrade. To me it seemed an extremely aristocratic and luxurious hotel. We were allocated large rooms with either two or three beds. There was a constant coming and going of civilians, Yugoslav soldiers, officers, students, and members of the Red Army. But no Germans, no Nazis, no swastikas! We could talk, laugh, and sing unhindered. The only thing we didn't know was what we should and would do. On the evening after our arrival there was a celebration in the hotel. The reason? There didn't need to be one; being alive was reason enough. Anyway, the Germans were in retreat and would lose the war. No one knew when the war would end, but that hardly seemed to matter. Music filled the various hotel ballrooms. There was dancing, plenty of good food, and even more to drink. The hotel corridors were full of people, the doors of most rooms were open, and friends, acquaintances, and strangers clinked glasses with everyone else. It was a celebration of life and hope. *Raki*, a potent aniseed-flavored liqueur, flowed endlessly. People drank from glasses, beakers, schnapps bottles, and water flasks. I had no experience with alcohol, but I joined in and drank to the health of whoever clinked my glass, each time taking a sip. As little as it was, it was still too much for me. My senses were clouded by the atmosphere of the evening, not least by the *raki*. This was the first and only time in my life that I got drunk. Some small part of my consciousness still functioned as I landed in my own room, threw up in waves, and collapsed on the bed.

We were kitted out in khaki uniforms like the British army, but our caps had a red-white-red cockade at the front. These small round badges indicated that we were Austrians. In addition to our uniforms we were given *Puschkas* — Russian machine pistols and ammunition. Some of our group had never held a weapon in their hands and nobody knew how to use a *Puschka*. Our first training was in a hotel room. Our "expert," H. S., demonstrated how to attach and remove the barrel, how to secure it, and how to remove the safety catch. During the demonstration the weapon went off and a shot bore into the floor, alarming all the other hotel guests; but we paid no notice as we were overcome by fits of laughter.

We were sent to training camp in Zemun, northwest of Belgrade. Two weeks had to suffice as our first engagement was scheduled for the end of January. That sounds manly and warlike, but in fact the plans and

In the Résistance

arrangements were grossly inefficient. The front was long and vague, and the idea was to push through to the Austrian border near Radkersburg and then join up with other Austrian groups in the region of Maribor, Celje, and Ljubljana to participate in the battle to liberate Austria. Almost all the elements needed to fulfill this mission were lacking. Moritz, the oldest among us, was responsible for the whole group. We had no military rank, so Moritz was the first among equals.

There were fourteen of us, including some youths and a Yugoslav driver. Our equipment consisted of a rickety open truck and a machine pistol and revolver for each of us. None of us except the driver, our Yugoslav comrade, spoke either Serbo-Croat or Hungarian. We had no knowledge of the region, insufficient information as to the constantly changing position of the front, and no real military training. During our first military exercise we discovered that most of the *Puschkas* were jammed; they simply did not function. Luckily we were not far from the town Novi Sad, where the guns could be repaired or exchanged. It was bitterly cold on the open platform of the truck and our blankets did little to warm us or keep out the icy wind. Our driver was quite young. To break the monotony of driving over poor country roads, for fun or simply to show off, he often drove too close to the farmers' carts, tipping them into the ditch at the side of the road. He either could not or chose not to understand our objections, as he did it again and again. Watching the farmer and his horses dragging themselves up and out of the ditch, he laughed and drove on.

From Novi Sad we passed through Batschka Topola to Senta in the northern part of Yugoslavia, close to the Hungarian border. There we were met by the mayor

Hitting Back

In uniform with "pushkas," in Novi Sad, (second from right)

and other local dignitaries. The accommodations were good, and we could at last wash, warm ourselves, rest, and change our clothes. In our honor there was a grand celebration dinner with copious amounts of fine food and no lack of drink. The aroma and taste of one particular dish we were served in Senta remains in my memory — goose roasted in pastry. While baking, the pastry was repeatedly pricked so that it absorbed the fat and juices, leaving the goose succulent and the pastry crisp. When I think of it today my mouth waters. I wonder if I'm so enthralled at the memory because it was a time of scarcity. In truth, it was singularly delicious and I have never had this dish since. Full and warmed by the alcohol, we slept long and soundly. Later we called it the "Battle of Senta."

In the Résistance

Our next stop was Subotica near the Hungarian border. We did some combat exercises, rested, and were provided with ammunition. We reckoned that we would soon encounter the enemy. We crossed the Yugoslav-Hungarian border and reached Baja, a small rustic town situated on a bend of the Danube. The town had already been liberated from German troops. The scene was dominated by Hungarian farmers and Russian (Red Army) soldiers. We reported to the local commander, but he didn't know what to do with us despite our papers and the efforts of Moritz and our Yugoslav driver. We had come peacefully, equipped with Russian *Puschkas* and reported to him, but he was suspicious of our uniforms. We spoke German and our red-white-red badges were meaningless to him. Finally, after examining our papers and stamps and after several telephone calls and discussions through an interpreter, he was willing to believe that we were not the enemy. But, he still had nothing for us to do. He would have preferred to send us back over the nearby border into Yugoslavia. However, eventually he allocated to us an empty farmhouse in which we could stay. It was the beginning of February and very cold. The paths, streets, and fields were covered with snow. Since we spoke neither Russian nor Hungarian, communication with the locals and the Russian soldiers was difficult. Some of the Hungarians could speak or understand German, but under the circumstances they preferred to pretend they couldn't. Baja should not have been more than a transitory stop, the plan being to cross the Danube to Pecs. But when we arrived in Baja, we discovered that the retreating Germans had blown up the bridges across the Danube. So reluctantly we had to wait in Baja. Our enthusiasm suddenly dissipated; we were disappointed and disheartened. Clearly our plan to travel via Pecs and Maribor to the Austrian border was no longer feasible.

We had no way of knowing that the destroyed bridges over the Danube had, in fact, saved us from certain death. The town of Pecs (Fünfkirchen) was the object of a fierce engagement. The German troops had dug themselves in, subsequently lost the town, and then regained it. We — all of fourteen men — would have run straight into the hands of the Nazi troops. It's not hard to imagine what would have been the outcome. Thank God for the blown-up bridges.

In reports about the First World War, you often read, "We lay in front of Verdun." I'm adapting this to: "We sat in Baja." But sitting was one thing, eating quite another. We were not Hungarian and did not belong to the Soviet army; we were neither internees nor prisoners of war. Who was responsible for providing us with food — which was in short supply anyway? We soon discovered that this small detail had escaped the notice of any authority. We tried our luck with the local farmers: a wasted effort as neither bread nor flour, eggs nor potatoes could be procured. At night we managed to steal turnips and two chickens — not much for fourteen young men. Moritz succeeded in coming up with a Soviet major who acknowledged that we needed food. The same day he sent us provisions: two thick slices of bacon and several cartons of coffee cubes, and nothing else. No bread and no potatoes. We wolfed down the bacon and drank the coffee. The next day we all had diarrhea. But that day, 12 February 1945, in our discomfort and misery, we remembered the events of 1934.[16] It was a humble reminder and we soon forgot our rumbling stomachs.

We tried in every possible way to make contact with the "right" people in Belgrade. Finally we succeeded.

In the Résistance

We were ordered "back to Belgrade." It was not at all difficult to leave Baja and we anticipated with pleasure the "flesh pots" of Yugoslavia. Towards the end of February we arrived in Belgrade fit and well. With no bridges, we had no battles and no wounds. We were alive and cheerful. The month of March passed with no particular events of note. Nothing dramatic happened, at least not concerning our small group.

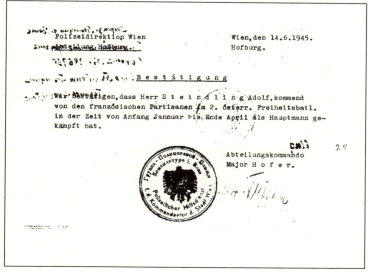

"Attestation ... Steindling Adolf, who had arrived from the French partisans, fought in the [Austrian] 2nd Freedom Battalion ..."

Back in Vienna

Although some of the German troops were still stationed in occupied countries, desperately defending themselves against total defeat, the war now really existed only within the boundaries of the Third Reich. The Americans, the British, and the French had pushed on to German soil. At the end of March, Soviet troops made their way along the Danube from Budapest towards Vienna and reached the city on April 13, 1945.[17] About that time we were flown from Belgrade to Papa, midway between Budapest and the Austrian border, where we joined up with units of the Red Army marching in the direction of Vienna. We travelled by truck from Papa via Sopron, Eisenstadt, and Laxenburg to Vienna.

What did I want, what did we want in Vienna? We could not imagine or had any idea what awaited us there. Had the whole effort, the long difficult journey and the risks that I had taken on myself been justified and necessary? Why did I have such thoughts when only a few kilometers separated me from my home town? I had left Vienna, my family and friends, almost seven years earlier. I had left behind me the city in which I had grown up and enjoyed a carefree youth. For seven years I dreamed, as did many others, of returning. For seven years Vienna was the focus of all my conversations with friends. The districts, the streets and parks, the coffee houses, dance bars, theaters, and cinemas, the sausage stalls selling *burenwurst*, the amusement park (Prater) and the Danube beaches, the memories of brawls and mischievous capers of my youth — a thousand other

In the Résistance

details — together they bound me to Vienna. What was I looking for now in Vienna? And what would I find? My parents and family were, thank God, not in this city. My friends from earlier days? They were either dispersed all over the world or had died in German concentration camps. Others had died as soldiers in the German army. And those that I could find in Vienna: are they Nazis, were they Nazis?

During the seven years of darkness, made up of seemingly infinite days and nights of fear — in Merxplas, St. Cyprien, Gurs, the Gestapo prison, the underground, the rolling cattle trucks — I (and not only I) thought of vengeance if we ever succeeded in defeating the Nazi monsters. Now, as we rolled towards Vienna,

Dolly Steindling, May 1945, in Vienna

Hitting Back

we heard a few lone shots by the northern rim of the city, disparate groups still fighting and the last nests of resistance being cleared away.

Did I still harbor thoughts of revenge? No, neither I nor my friends felt the need to wreak revenge.

> *Combatting a hated murderous regime, fighting against its representatives and executive organs, against cold-blooded murderers in uniform or civilian clothing had nothing to do with striking in blind rage against people who had fallen into our hands or accidentally stepped in front of our machine guns. Now, in the hours and days of their defeat and collapse — our liberation and resurrection — they were the ones living in bombed-out ruins, hungry and full of fear. To take revenge upon these people, to demonstrate our power, to spread fear, to stage executions would mean using the same Fascist methods. Surely I had not spent years fighting against all forms of Fascism to do that. Yet, at the same time, I believe firmly in the prosecution, condemnation, and perhaps even the physical extermination of murderers, mass murderers, and Fascist criminals, irrespective of their names, standing, rank, or nationality.*

The nearer we came to the city limits of Vienna the more difficult the journey became. Buildings and factories, streets and houses, had been ripped apart by bombs. Rubble was everywhere and it was impossible to drive. Burst water and gas pipes and piles of rubbish added to the chaos. I never imagined my homecoming to be like this. Continually our truck had to alter its route and so it took hours to get from Inzersdorf, on the southern outskirts of the city, through the tenth and the fourth districts to the center. Our journey ended in the Seidengasse in Vienna's seventh district. We were provisionally accommodated in an empty flat in the Schottenfeldsgasse. What now? On this day the answer sounded flat and banal: participate in the reconstruction of Vienna and Austria and establish a new democratic republic.

I began to wander through Vienna, particularly the ninth district: Schultz-Strassnitzky-Gasse, our former home. Glasergasse, Seegasse, Rotenlöwengasse, Rossauerlände, and the "Promsch" — our neighborhood. I moved as if through a ghost town. There were no children, no young people, no grown-ups, no old people. Where were the people who had lived in these streets, had sat in the parks and filled the city with life? I entered houses, knocked on doors, and asked about friends. What I found were not my former friends or

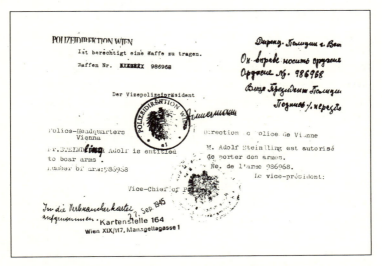

"Adolf Steindling is entitled to bear arms" by the Russian, American, and French occupation police authorities in Vienna, 1945.

Hitting Back

school colleagues, but worn-out women, mostly mothers. I learned that Gerti P. and Franz H. had died in battle; Fritz B. was with the SS, Lois R. with the SA. I soon gave up my search for friends. It appeared that my generation no longer existed.

I rang the bell of our former neighbors who lived at number 12, acquaintances and friends of the family. The encounters were overwhelmingly distressing. With minor variations the conversations were almost all the same. First came the attempt to apologize for what had happened, together with the assurance that they themselves had nothing to do with it and, of course, did not know what really had happened. Then a short report on the misfortune of their own family, including the fact that members of the family who had joined the SS, the SA or the SD, had perhaps erred in their choices. This was invariably followed by complaints about the bombings, the lack of food, rationing, and the black market. In effect, they were not conversations but monologues for which I was a road-weary and unwilling listener. There were hardly any questions about *my* parents or *my* family, where *I* had been all these years, how *I* had survived or how and why *I* had returned to Vienna. They found the fact that I was still alive a reproach that filled them with discomfort, if not fear.

I did not knock on the door of our apartment, 12/6 Schultz-Strassnitzky-Gasse. I did not want to know who was living there, in the rooms where I grew up with my family. Nor did I venture to our shop in the Seegasse.

The physical ruin of the houses and the debris in the streets did not disturb me nearly as much as the human ruins — the moral rubble — from which I could not escape in my beloved Vienna.

In the Résistance

Dolly Steindling at the time of writing his memoirs

Epilogue

In the introduction to his memoirs, Dolly Steindling described his first years in Vienna after the war:

> *I still had to suffer privations as far as money, food and clothing were concerned. But I was full of idealism for the reconstruction of a new and better Austria. I wanted to participate in establishing a more just society and to help ensure that later generations would never have to suffer similar sorrows and humiliations. Immediately after the end of the war in May 1945 I had an active, leading role in the creation and development of a new youth organization, the F.Ö.J, the "Free Austrian Youth." I was frequently, almost constantly together with young people, girls and boys. We worked and discussed by day and often far into the night. Lasting friendships developed.*

Heading the Communist youth at a parade in Vienna (third from left)

Epilogue

But disillusion was not long in coming, and one of the most far-reaching was the following:

At the beginning of 1946 I was officially allocated an apartment in a small house in Wegerer street in the 19th district of Vienna. The apartment was empty; it had belonged to a Nazi dignitary and his wife who had fled. After 1948 he considered the political situation to be safe enough and returned from the security of western Austria. He appealed to court to regain possession of the apartment and the court decided in his favor. What more needs to be said?

Married, with a small daughter and his wife eight months pregnant, Dolly Steindling had to find new lodgings for his growing family. This was possible through the intervention of a friend who was prepared to forego his own rights on the allocation of an apartment.

Dolly Steindling was then, in his own words, "a young man with much idealism and enthusiasm but without a profession, commercial knowledge or experience, and without any studied or acquired skills." After two years in the leadership of the "Free Austrian Youth," he began to take courses in labor law, which led him to the position of personnel manager in a major industrial enterprise. In 1956, a year after Austria regained full independence, he entered the "Central Wechselstuben A.G.," a small bank that had been founded in 1918 by the Hungarian monarchical government and now belonged to the Finance Ministry of the People's Republic of Hungary. Because there was no official agreement between Austria and Hungary, the bank was staffed with Austrians and was officially managed as an Austrian institution. A very modest financial concern, it was comprised of nine employees in all, including two directors. Now, thirty-eight years old, the hardworking and eager Dolly Steindling contributed largely to the dynamic development of the bank. By 1964, when the Director General announced his retirement, Dolly was virtually the leading figure in the enterprise. But at that point he was to be disillusioned once again, this time by the highest authorities of the Finance Ministry of Communist Hungary:

> *Indirectly I discovered that the Hungarian Finance Ministry was looking for a new Director General both by recommendation and through newspaper advertisements in Austria and West Germany. One of those who were approached, a director of an Austrian bank, told me himself of the offer and that he had refused. He also indicated to the Hungarians that in his opinion I was suitable for the position. In spring 1964 I was visited by the head of the appointment section of the Hungarian Finance Ministry for a first official discussion on the question of succession. At first he was very flattering about the quality and diversity of my work and how my diligence was appreciated. Then came the solicitous statement that they could not demand of me that I take over the commercial management in addition to all my other duties. Finally came the announcement that they were forced to look for a new Director General outside the bank, together with the claim that I would surely appreciate this.*
>
> *He did not describe the requisite qualifications that a new Director General should bring to the position, but the sentence fell: "It must be someone with a green hat, a traditional Styrian hat...." This green hat was naturally meant as a symbol and signified no less than that a Styrian hat would not suit a Jew with left-wing political leanings and*

Epilogue

a past in the Résistance movement against the Nazis. In other words, a managing director of a bank in Vienna, irrespective of the fact that this bank is owned by Hungary, cannot be a Jew and must not have a past such as mine — in order not to irritate anyone in Austria.

My reaction to the section head of the Ministry was clear and unequivocal. I would accept unconditionally any new superior who could work for the good of the bank... and from whom I could learn. I would rather be number two or number three in a flourishing bank than number one in a second-rate bank. Were he only to be a "green hat," then although I was no longer that young I would look for a new job.

Dolly Steindling did not have to look for another job. In 1964 he became the Director and later Director General of the Central Wechsel und Credit Bank A.G., as the bank became known, and very soon transformed the still small financial enterprise into a flourishing bank. He headed the institution until 1982. Upon his retirement his successors in the management of the bank recognized that "...under his leadership the bank experienced a particularly successful development." The multitude of bankers, financial leaders and high ranking officials, Austrians and foreigners, who honored the bank in 1978 when it celebrated its sixtieth anniversary bore evidence to this assertion. By then the number of its employees exceeded one hundred.

Dolly Steindling's disenchantment with the New Austria he had endeavored to help build was followed by a slow but sure distancing from his previous enthusiasm for Communism. The final blow in this respect was the attitude of the Soviet Union towards the State of Israel in the 1967 Middle East crisis. Moscow's support and later protection of the Arab aggressors — in a conflict that was aimed at the destruction of Israel — added to his already existing criticism of Soviet politics. His support for the Jewish state from then on was open and unflinching.

Fascism and anti-Semitism remained his major concerns. While writing his memoirs in September 1980, he noted the following:

> *I am writing about the past. Personal experience was bound inseparably with the suffering of millions of people caused by Fascism and the war. Most people do not want to know about that period, and they close their eyes to the present as well — but the past catches up with us. The question that I sometime ask myself: whether or not I acted correctly, I always answer with a resounding "Yes." I am now more convinced of this than ever. Over the past months much has become clear that had been hidden for years and tolerated by various democratic governments, including the Social Democrats: the growth of neo-Fascist and neo-Nazi organizations. This includes activities, demonstrations, slogans, and hatred propaganda. It is too reminiscent of the time we thought could never be repeated: 1932–1938. Prosperity scantily disguises it.*

Less than three years later, Dolly Steindling succumbed to the fatal illness that he had suffered from for several years. According to his doctor's diagnosis, his intensive and continuous exposure to X-rays during his clandestine surgery in 1943 largely contributed to this condition.

Dolly Steindling lost fourteen members of his mother's family in the Holocaust. One of his cousins, Sheinka Schechter, returned to Tarnow after having studied medicine in Vienna. There she joined the

Epilogue

underground movement, was caught by the Nazis, and executed in the town's central square. His parents, sister, and brother-in-law, four of his maternal cousins, and his father's brother's family, were saved by their timely immigration to Israel, then Palestine.

Haim Avni

*A monument in Tarnow, Poland
(the home town of the author's father),
in memory of 800 Jewish children murdered on June 11, 1942.
(courtesy of Yad Vashem, Jerusalem)*

Notes

INTRODUCTION:

1. Kenneth Jacobson, *Embattled Selves, An Investigation into the Nature of Identity, Through Oral Histories of Holocaust Survivors* (New York: Atlantic Monthly Press, 1994). Starting early in 1978 and over the course of some four years, Jacobson interviewed and recorded "nearly 300 men and women." Fifteen of these stories are included in his book (p. 9). Dolly Steindling's was not among them.
2. *Maquis* - literally bush; synonym for rural guerrillas in France whose bases were in the hilly and mountainous bushlands.
3. Erich Maria Remarque, *The Arch of Triumph* (1945). A film with Ingrid Bergman, Charles Boyer and Charles Laughton, based on the novel, brought this theme to the attention of a wide public.
4. Elsbeth Kasser, "Mein Leben im Lager Gurs," in: *Gurs, Ein Internierungslager in Südfrankreich, 1939–1943: Zeichnungen, Aquarelle, Fotografien. Sammlung Elsbeth Kasser* (Denmark: Viborg, 1991), the catalogue of the exhibition. See on p. 50: a partial bibliography, 20 items on the camp. Anne Grynberg, *Les Camps de la Honte, Les Internés Juifs des Camps Français (1939–1944)* (Editions La Découverte; Paris 1991), tells the story of all the French camps, featuring Gurs as the most central.
5. *Dokumentationsarchiv des österreichischen Wiederstandes* (hereafter DÖW) file 6564. Otto Niebergall to Tilly Marek (Spiegel), July 14, 1970.
6. Fritz Molden, *Die Feuer in der Nacht, Opfer und Sinn des österreichischen Wiederstandes 1938–1945* (Vienna: Amalthea Verlag, 1988), pp. 24–25, 107–35.

Notes

7. Tilly Spiegel, *Österreicher in der belgischen und französischen Resistance* (Vienna: Europa Verlag, 1969). Two earlier works by the same author are also included in this publication.
8. Kristina Schewig-Pfoser and Ernst Schwager, "Österreicher in der Resistance," in: DÖW, *Österreicher im Exil, Frankreich 1938–1945. Eine Dokumentation* (Vienna: Österreichischer Bundesverlag, 1984; with an introduction by Prime Minister Bruno Kreisky), pp. 25–31, documents pp. 177–239.
9. *Ibid.*, Josef Meisel, pp. 191–95; Elizabeth Eidinger, pp. 196–99.
10. Spiegel, *Österreicher in der belgischen und französischen Resistance*, pp. 39–47.
11. Alois Peter, *et al.* (editors), *Österreicher im Spanischen Bürgerkrieg, Interbrigadisten berichten über ihre Erlebnisse, 1936 bis 1945* (Vienna: Österreichischer Budesverlag, 1986; historical surveys by Alois Peter, pp. 11–37, 61–71, 245–64); Heinrich Fritz, *Stationen meines Lebens* (Vienna: Globus Verlag, 1990), pp. 109–30.
12. Anny Latour, *La Résistance juive en France (1940–1944)* (Paris: Stock, 1970), pp. 226–310; Alain Michel, *Les Eclaireurs Israélites de France Pendant la Seconde Guerre Mondiale* (Paris: Édition des EIF, 1994), pp. 189–90.
13. Molden, *Die Feuer*, pp. 153–58
14. Max Goldberger, "Vom Maquis zu den jugoslawischen Partisanen," in: Peter, *et al., Österreicher im Spanischen Bürgerkrieg*, pp. 289–91. This testimony requires substantiation since beginning May 1943 official relations between Great Britain and Tito were very close.
15. Arnold Paucker, "Resistance of German and Austrian Jews to the Nazi Regime 1933–1945," *Leo Baeck Institute Year Book*, Vol. XL (1995): 1–19.
16. DÖW, File 2616 I, II, III, Tilly Marek (Spiegel) to Yad Vashem, mid-August 1965.
17. Anne Grynberg (Coordination), *Les Juifs dans la Résistance*

et la Libération. Histoire, temoignages, débats (Paris: Édition du Scribe, 1985), pp. 49–57. *Ibid.*, p. 16, the quotation from Bloch's will, written on 18 March 1941 and published in his posthumous *L'Etrange défaite* (Paris: Alain Michel, 1957), pp. 223–24.

18. Lucien Lazare, *Rescue as Resistance. How Jewish Organizations Fought the Holocaust in France* (New York: Columbia University Press, 1996), p. 277, quoting Lucien Steinberg, *La révolte des justes* (Paris: Fayard, 1970), p. 146.

19. Renée Poznanski, "A Methodological Approach to the Study of Jewish Resistance in France," *Yad Vashem Studies*, Vol. XVIII (1987): 1–39; André Kaspi, "Un bilan provisoire," in: *Les Juifs de France dans la Seconde Guerre Mondiale* (Pardés 16; Paris: Le Cerf, 1992), p. 15.

20. Main d'Oeuvre Immigrée (M.O.I.) was established by the French Communist party in 1925 as Main d'Oeuvre Etrangere in order to incorporate the numerous immigrant national groups. It was renamed M.O.I. in 1932 and many of its members were the earliest Communist Resistance fighters. Lazare, *Rescue as Resistance*, pp. 279–81. Anny Kriegel, the well-known historian and sociologist who in 1942–44 was an active member of the Jeunesse Communiste Juive, the clandestine Jewish Communist youth organization, underlines this fact in "Resistants communistes et Juifs persecutés" in her *Réflexion sur les questions Juives* (Paris: Hachette, 1984), pp. 15–18 and particularly pp. 46–47. See also Henry H. Weinberg, "Defining Jewish Resistance in France," *Midstream* Vol. XXXVIII No. 6 (August-September 1992): 15–18. Annette Wieviorka, *Ils étaient Juifs, resistants, communistes* (Paris: Denoel, 1986) and Stephane Courtois, Denis Peschanski, Adam Rayski, *Le sang de l'étranger, Les immigrés de la MOI dans la Résistance* (Paris: Fayard, 1989) dealt extensively with the history of the Jewish units in the M.O.I.

21. Henri Michel, *La guerre de l'ombre* (Paris: Grasset, 1970), p. 170, quoted by Lazare, *Rescue as Resistance*, p. 276.

Notes

22. Grynberg, *Les Juifs dans la Résistance*, pp. 45–46.
23. *Ibid.*, 47–48.
24. Michael R. Marrus and Robert P. Paxton, *Vichy France and the Jews* (New York: Schocken Books, 1981), pp. 189–90.
25. Grynberg, *Les Juifs dans la Résistance*, p. 54.

REFUGEE:

1. "Kristallnacht," the nationwide burning of synagogues and attacks on Jewish public buildings, shops, and homes on November 9–10, 1938, was preceded in Vienna by the systematic and brutal expulsion of Jews from their homes. The "operation" began on the eve of Yom Kippur, October 5, and continued throughout that month. See Herbert Rosenkranz, *Der Novemberpogrom 1938 in Wien, Historisches Museum der Stadt Wien*, (1988), pp. 2–3. According to an official German report on the results of the Kristallnacht in Vienna, 7,800 Jews were arrested, most of them taken to Dachau concentration camp; 42 synagogues were destroyed; 4,083 shops closed and their property confiscated; and 680 Jews committed suicide. See Leni Yahil, *The Holocaust, the Fate of European Jewry 1932–1945*, Vol. I (New York: Oxford University Press, 1990), p. 111. "The night of the long knives" refers to June 30, 1934, when, upon Hilter's orders, the SS attacked and slaughtered hundreds of its own followers and particularly members of the SA, the Nazi stormtroopers headed by Ernst Roehm.
2. "Hashomer Hatzair," the Zionist, left-of-center socialist youth movement, steered its members towards emigration to Palestine and agricultural settlement in kibbutzim.
3. The author uses the term *Kultusgemeinde* here and in other places to refer to the local Jewish-organized community. The *Israelitische Kultusgemeinde* in Vienna was the comprehensive Jewish institution, officially recognized by law, that *inter alia* was in charge of the official registration of Jewish

Hitting Back

weddings and births and the maintenance of the Jewish cemetery, along with other functions, including charity, education, and official political representation. These were not necessarily the functions of the Jewish institutions to which the author turned for help in Switzerland, France, and Belgium, but he refers to them consistently as "the Jewish Community." Swiss Jewry (18,000 in 1933), organized since 1904 under the *Schweizerischer Israelitischer Gemeindebund* (SIG), had its headquarters in Zurich and provided help to the refugees through its affiliate *Verein schweizerischer israelitischer Armenpfleger* (VSIA). In 1938 the American Jewish Joint Distribution Committee (AJDC) began to contribute partly to that work. See Yehuda Bauer, *My Brother's Keeper* (Philadelphia: The Jewish Publication Society of America, 1974), pp. 172–73, 175–76.

4. "The Jewish Community" in this case must have been the *Comité d'Assistance aux Réfugiés* (CAR), established in June 1936 and under the auspices of one of the Rothschilds, the chief rabbi, and others; its president was Albert Levy. It was the major organization of French Jewry for the support of refugees, although by no means the only one. Starting in 1938 the AJDC contributed vast funds to CAR: US$ 130,884 in that year and $589,000 in 1939. See Grynberg, *Les Camps de la Honte,* pp. 108–11; Bauer, *My Brother's Keeper,* pp. 264–65.

5. "The Jewish Community" of Brussels eventually became the aid committee headed by Max Gottschalk, which provided support to the refugees and helped their emigration on behalf of HICEM (HIAS-JCA-EMIGDIREKT). The JDC supplied a considerable portion of the funding. The author was among the 3,000 refugees who illegally entered Belgium from November 1938 to the end of that year. See Bauer, *My Brother's Keeper,* pp. 172, 265–66. His brother was among the 3,000 refugees who were brought to the "Kitchner Camp for Poor Persons" at Richborough, Kent. See Bauer, ibid. p. 271; Bernard Wasserstein, *Britain and the Jews*

Notes

   of Europe 1939–1945 (Oxford: Clarendon Press, 1979), p. 10. He was later admitted to the United States.
6. Saint Cyprien, like Argelès and other places in the region of Département des Pyrénées-Orientales, was designated in February 1939 by the French Government as the location of a temporary concentration camp for the defeated soldiers of the Spanish Republic. By March 1939 tens of thousands of Spanish refugees were held there in the most appalling conditions. The camp was officially closed on December 19, 1940 "for sanitation reasons" after the Jewish inmates had been transferred, in October of that year, to Gurs. See Grynberg, *Les Camps de la Honte*, pp. 40–41, 156.
7. The decision to join the return transport to Belgium was taken by the leaders of the Communist group. When Franz Soel, whose mother was also interned in Saint Cyprien, did not obey the decision, he was ostracized (his oral testimony, August 1997). If indeed the repatriation was meant to apply only to "Aryans," the French were not very strict in their selection.
8. This episode coincided with the one described by Marrus and Paxton, *Vichy France and the Jews*, p. 10: "on 8 August Polizeimajor Walter Krueger in Bordeaux sent 1400 German Jews across the demarcation line ... The French locked them up in the camp at Saint Cyprien...." The naiveté of at least some of the German Jews was evidenced by their appeal to the German Foreign Office for help against the French authorities for their treatment that, in their opinion, was an insult to Germany.
9. Before starting her work at Gurs (on December 20, 1940), Elsbeth Kasser represented the *Cartel Suisse de Secours aux Enfants de la Guerre* in southern France. A nurse by profession, she had served with Swiss aid agencies during the civil war in Spain and in a physicians' mission to Finland during the war against Russia (1939–40). See Kasser, "Mein Leben im Lager Gurs," p. 8; Grynberg, *Les Camps de la Honte*, p. 190.

10. The correct title is: *Der Teufel in Frankreich* (Rudolfstadt: Freifen Verlag, 1945). See the English version: *The Devil in France, my Encounter with him in the Summer of 1940* (London: Hutchinson & Co), pp. 21–22.
11. Krausian refers to followers of Karl Christian Friedrich Krause (1781–1832), who developed the concept of "union of mankind" as part of his "panentheism," based on both pantheism and theism.
12. The OSE (OZE) was founded in Russia in 1912 as a society for the protection of the health of Jews (*Obschchestvo Zdravookhraneniya Yevreyev*) and was active in Eastern Europe and France during the inter-war period. Relief and child care were its main activities in France.
13. Abbot (Abbé) Alexander Glasberg, a converted Ukrainian Jew, served a small parish in Lyon. With approval of the Archbishop of Lyon, Cardinal Gerlier, he became active on behalf of the internees of the French concentration camps. He mounted an extraordinarily efficient relief and rescue network. Ninon Hait, who, with several other activists comprised Glasberg's team, was an active leader of the underground relief and rescue organization set up by the Jewish Scouts of France (*Eclaireurs Israélites de France*, EIF) called "La Sixième." See Lazare, *L'Abbé Glasberg* (Paris: Le Cerf, 1990); Latour, *La Résistance juive*, pp. 52–53, 72–73; Alain Michel, *Les Eclaireurs Israélites de France*, pp. 165–76.
14. The *Deuxième Bureau*, The French Armed Forces' intelligence service, was the backbone of the liaison of Charles de Gaulle's Free French Movement (later, the French National Committee) with the Gaullist armed resistance organizations from London, where he had arrived in June 1940, until his return to France in August 1944. Charles de Gaulle, *Mémoires de Guerre* (Paris: Plon, 1954), Vol. I, p. 87; Vol II, pp. 305–13.
15. ORT, the Organization for Rehabilitation through Training, was established in Russia and extended its activities after World War I to Eastern Europe and France. It was

Notes

supported by international ORT set up in the United States. During the war a considerable part of its budget in France was provided by the JDC.

IN THE RÉSISTANCE:

1. "Genuine" papers were false papers carrying names and personal details of persons who were indeed registered in one of the French municipalities and could be corroborated when the police or the Gestapo cross-checked the validity of these papers by phoning the municipality in which they were issued. "False-false" papers were without such a backing.
2. Franz Marek was one of the three leaders of *Travail Allemand* in northern France. He was arrested in Paris in August 1944 and was liberated during the uprising and liberation of the city. He was a member of the Austrian Communist politburo. DÖW 2626 I, testimony by Tilly Spiegel-Marek.
3. Otto Heller was the author of *Der Untergang des Judentums* (The Ruin of Judaism), published in 1931, in which he predicted the complete assimilation of the Jews in western countries and their survival, as a national entity, in the Soviet Union. His work had a great impact on Jewish Communist youth. He was active in the *Résistance* in southern France from the beginning of the war, imprisoned, escaped, and managed to infiltrate one of the German bases in Lille, acting as a translator. His wife and daughter, who were active in the underground movement in Lyon, were caught by the Germans, taken to Ravensbrück concentration camp, and survived the war. See DÖW 2626 I, Spiegel, *Österreicher in der belgischen und französischen Résistance*, pp. 43–44.
4. BDM (*Bund deutscher Mädel*), the female Nazi youth movement officially established in 1930, trained its girls to

become proud, physically strong, and prolific German mothers. Racist indoctrination was a major feature of their education.

5. Ernst Wexberg managed to escape after sixty days in prison. After two weeks of hiding in the courtyard of a Frenchman in July 1943, he went to Paris and Lyon. He was one of those who were ordered by the Austrian Resistance to return to Vienna disguised as a "foreign worker." He was caught, taken to concentration camps and liberated in Theresienstadt. See Spiegel, *Österreicher in der belgischen und französischen Resistance,* p. 60.

6. British soldiers of the S.O.E. (Special Operations Executive [the commando unit for activities behind enemy lines]) were active in the region where "Jean Obrecht" was caught. Headed by their commander, Michael Totobas ("Capitaine Michel"), they successfully derailed many German trains. On the night of June 27, 1943, during the period when Dolly Steindling was interrogated and tortured by the Gestapo, they attacked a major locomotive plant in Lille, hitting one of their largest targets. See M. R. D. Foot, *S.O.E. in France* (London, 1966), p. 264.

7. After serving as the liaison agent of the *Travail Allemand* with the French *Résistance* in the Pas-de-Calais zone in northern France, Turl Schnierer ("René") went to Vienna disguised as a French "foreign worker" in the German war industries. He was also discovered and imprisoned in August 1944. Tilly Spiegel listed him as a "traitor" because, according to her, without being tortured, he mentioned to the Gestapo one of his comrades they did not know about. He was deported to Auschwitz, from there to Sachsenhauen concentration camp near Berlin, and later to Buchenwald, where he was liberated. He died in August 1945. See DÖW 2626 I, Tilly Spiegel's lists sent to Yad Vashem.

8. The "Bund," founded in 1897 in Vilna (Lithuania, then part of the Russian Empire), acquired a leading role

Notes

among the Jewish proletarians in Russia before the Russian Revolution, and in Poland in the inter-war period. It was also influential among the Jewish emigrants in western countries.

9. The French novelist Henri Barbusse, laureate of the prestigious *Prix Goncourt* for his *Le Feu, Journal d'une éscouade* (in English, *Under Fire*, 1917), in which he described soldiers' life in the trenches during World War I, was famous for his pacifism. After 1918 he became one of the leading Communist writers in France.

10. Walter Ardel had infiltrated the German air force base Bron, near Lyon, where he was responsible for purchasing various items of equipment. Large sums of German money passed through his hands, some of which he diverted to the *Résistance*. He was arrested on the day that he intended to conclude a major financial operation, abandon his position, and join a *maquis*. See Spiegel, *Österreicher in der belgischen und französischen Résistance*, p. 44.

11. In addition to his position as head of the SS, Gestapo, and Waffen SS, which he had held previously, after the failed attempt on Hilter's life, Heinrich Himmler was given the command of the reserve units of the army and of the army group Vistula. See Lionel Kochan, "Himmler, Heinrich," *Encyclopedia of the Holocaust* (London: MacMillan, 1990), Vol. II, p. 661.

12. The call to the Austrian prisoners of war to volunteer for military service on the side of the Allies included the patriotic argument of securing for Austria the fulfillment of the Allies' promise to recognize Austria's independence. However, the pamphlets distributed among them contained also very clear marks of leftist ideology pointing to what liberated Austria should be. See "An die österreichischen Kriegsgefangenen!" DÖW 19.005 printed in *Österreicher im Exil*, pp. 235–37. The efforts of the Austrian officer Arthur Huschak, recipient of a high French *Résistance* decoration, to raise two Austrian battalions from among the Austrian

POWs also failed. On the other hand he has been reported to have succeeded, together with another two individuals, in the "quick and without bureaucratic investigations" release of some 60,000 such prisoners, averting their eventual recruitment to the French Foreign Legion. See Spiegel, *Österreicher in der belgischen und französischen Résistance,* pp. 26–27.

13. The decision to send many Austrian activists of *Travail Allemand* back to Vienna, followed by several successful operations by the Gestapo — the case of Oskar Grossman in Lyon, another in June 1944 in Paris, as well as others in August — decimated the Austrian resistance movement in France. See DÖW 2616 I–III, Tilly Spiegel's notes to the printed material. Note 3 (the case of Paula Draxler) and 14.

14. The reference is to Harry Spiegel and his wife Irene. Their contacts with Yugoslav and French comrades from the International Brigades in Spain were evidently the background to this whole episode. See DÖW 2626 I, II, III, Tilly Spiegel (C. Namenregister, p. 4).

15. Moritz Fels-Margulies, one of the older members in the group of Austrian internees at St. Cyprien and Gurs, was later taken to other concentration camps in France. He was imprisoned in Castres, from which he broke out in October 1943 with the other thirty-six prisoners. He was again caught by the Gestapo in early August 1944 in Paris and on the night of August 21 managed to escape with other deportees from the last train that left Drancy concentration camp in Paris on its way to the east. See DÖW 2745b, his testimony (partly published in *Österreicher im Exil,* pp. 180–81).

16. On February 12, 1934, and for the following three days, the right-wing Dolfuss government brutally suppressed the strike and armed uprising of the Social Democrat party in Austria.

17. The Red Army's offensive towards Austria began in mid-

Notes

March 1945 in Hungary, and on March 27 the Russian troops were reported to have reached within sixty miles of Vienna. On April 7 they crossed the Danube and penetrated the Austrian capital, but it took another six days until fighting in the streets began. See Robert Goralski, *World War II Almanac 1931–1945, A Political and Military Record* (New York: Bonanza Books, 1985), pp. 388–89, 393, 396.